English Literature:

A Mirror of Indian Consciousness-How Indian minds reflect and refract the English tongue

English Literature: A Mirror of Indian Consciousness

Published By: Wissira Research Lab

Imprint Name: Wissira Press

US Office: Carmel, United States- 46074

India Office: KDP, RNE, India-201017

Email: editor@wissira.us,

Website: https://books.wissira.us

Mobile: +91 7535 916 555

Dr. Jyoti Devi

ISBN

978-93-7559-834-3 Digital (delivered electronically)

978-93-7559-090-3 Paperback / softback

Maharaja Agrasen Himalayan Garhwal University,

Address: Uttarakhand, India

Edition: 2026

Printed In: India

Maharaja Agrasen Himalayan Garhwal University,

Address: Uttarakhand, India

English Literature:

A Mirror of Indian Consciousness-

How Indian minds reflect and refract the English tongue

2026

Author:

Dr. Jyoti Devi

Maharaja Agrasen Himalayan Garhwal University,

Address: Uttarakhand, India

Published By

Wissira Research Lab

ISBN 978-93-7559-090-3

9 789375 590903

Preface

English literature in India is not merely a reflection of linguistic adoption; it is a testimony to the evolving consciousness of a civilization negotiating history, identity, and modernity. English Literature: A Mirror of Indian Consciousness - How Indian Minds Reflect and Refract the English Tongue emerges from the recognition that English, once introduced through colonial structures, has been reimagined and reshaped by Indian writers to articulate indigenous experiences, emotions, and philosophies.

The presence of English in India cannot be understood only as a historical consequence of colonial rule; it must also be seen as a space of creative negotiation. Over time, Indian writers did not simply inherit the English language—they inhabited it, questioned it, stretched its boundaries, and infused it with local rhythms, metaphors, and worldviews. In doing so, they transformed a language of power into a language of expression, resistance, and self-definition. English became a tool not of erasure, but of articulation—capable of voicing social realities, spiritual introspection, ethical dilemmas, and cultural memory rooted deeply in the Indian experience.

The Indian engagement with English has never been passive. From its early encounters with colonial education to its contemporary global expressions, English in India has functioned as a site of dialogue—between tradition and change, local and global, self and society. Indian writers have transformed English into a medium capable of carrying cultural memory, social critique, spiritual inquiry, and personal introspection. This book seeks to trace that journey by examining how Indian consciousness has continuously redefined the English language.

Rather than treating Indian English literature as a derivative tradition, this work positions it as an active, evolving intellectual and artistic movement. The Indian writer writing in English stands at a unique crossroads—shaped by multiple histories, languages, and cultural inheritances. This hybridity gives rise to literature that is neither wholly Western nor conventionally indigenous, but profoundly Indian in sensibility, thought, and emotional depth.

The chapters of this book are organized thematically to highlight the multiple dimensions of Indian English literature. Beginning with the historical encounter between English and the Indian mind, the discussion moves through questions of identity, cultural negotiation, and literary sensibility. It explores poetry, prose, drama, feminist writing, postcolonial resistance, and diasporic narratives, culminating in an examination of contemporary voices and emerging directions. Each chapter emphasizes how English becomes Indian not by imitation but by adaptation and reinterpretation.

Ultimately, this work affirms that Indian English literature is a living, dynamic field—one that continues to evolve alongside social change and global interaction. By examining how Indian minds reflect and refract the English tongue, this book invites readers to engage with literature as a mirror of consciousness, creativity, and cultural resilience—revealing how language, when reshaped by lived experience, becomes a powerful expression of identity and thought.

Author:

Dr. Jyoti Devi

Overview of the Book

English Literature: A Mirror of Indian Consciousness – How Indian Minds Reflect and Refract the English Tongue offers a comprehensive exploration of how English, once introduced as a colonial language, has been transformed into a powerful medium of Indian self-expression. The book examines Indian English literature not as an imitation of Western models but as a distinct literary tradition shaped by India's history, culture, philosophy, and social realities.

The book begins by situating English within the historical context of colonial India, explaining how education, administration, and intellectual exchange brought English into close contact with the Indian mind. It highlights how Indian thinkers and writers responded creatively to this encounter, gradually reshaping English to articulate indigenous concerns. From this foundation, the book moves into an analysis of language and identity, showing how English became a space for cultural negotiation, hybridity, and self-definition.

Subsequent chapters explore how Indian consciousness finds expression across major literary genres. Prose writing is examined as a medium that captures social realities, ethical dilemmas, and everyday life, while poetry in English is discussed as a reflection of India's inner, spiritual, and emotional world. Drama in English is presented as a socially engaged form that brings issues of reform, justice, and collective awareness to the public stage.

The book also addresses critical perspectives such as postcolonial resistance and feminist consciousness, demonstrating how English has been used to challenge power structures, patriarchy, and historical marginalization. Diasporic and transnational writings are analysed to show how migration and globalization further reshape Indian identity, producing layered and hybrid forms of consciousness. The final chapters focus on contemporary Indian English literature, highlighting new voices, emerging themes, and the impact of digital culture and regional diversity.

Overall, the book presents Indian English literature as a dynamic and evolving field that mirrors the complexities of Indian society. It emphasizes that English in India is no longer a foreign or elite language, but an Indian language enriched by local experiences and global interactions. Designed for students, educators, and researchers, the book provides a structured, accessible, and critical overview of how Indian minds continue to reflect and refract the English tongue in meaningful and innovative ways.

Table of Contents

1

English and the Indian Mind – A Historical Encounter

1.1 Arrival of English in the Indian Subcontinent

This section traces the introduction of the English language in India through trade, administration, and education. English initially entered Indian society as a functional language of governance and commerce but gradually expanded into intellectual and cultural spaces. Indians encountered English not merely as a foreign tongue but as a new system of thought that interacted with indigenous traditions of learning.

The arrival of the English language in the Indian subcontinent was closely linked to the expansion of British political and commercial interests from the seventeenth century onward. English first gained a foothold through the activities of the British East India Company, which established trading posts along the Indian coastline. In its early phase, English functioned primarily as a practical medium used in trade negotiations, administrative records, and communication between colonial officials and local intermediaries. At this stage, it remained largely confined to commercial and bureaucratic domains rather than everyday social life.

As British control gradually expanded, English acquired a more institutional role in governance and law. The colonial administration introduced English in courts, revenue systems, and official correspondence, making it a language associated with authority and power. This administrative usage brought Indian elites into closer contact with English, especially those involved in legal, clerical, or diplomatic roles. For many Indians, learning English became a means of social mobility, enabling access to employment and influence within the colonial structure.

The most transformative phase in the spread of English occurred through education. The introduction of English-medium instruction in schools and colleges-particularly after the nineteenth century-positioned English as a language of modern knowledge. Subjects such as science, philosophy, and history were increasingly taught in English, exposing Indian learners to Western intellectual traditions.

This educational shift did not replace indigenous systems entirely but interacted with classical learning in Sanskrit, Persian, and regional languages, creating a complex intellectual exchange.

Over time, English moved beyond its functional origins and entered India's cultural and literary consciousness. Indian thinkers and writers began to engage with English not simply as a foreign language but as a tool for self-expression and debate. They adapted it to articulate Indian realities, social concerns, and philosophical ideas. Thus, the arrival of English in India was not a one-directional imposition but a dynamic process in which the language was reshaped by Indian experiences, ultimately becoming an important medium for cultural reflection and creative expression.

1.2 Colonial Education and Intellectual Transformation

English education reshaped Indian intellectual life by introducing Western philosophy, science, and literary forms. While colonial policies aimed to create administrative intermediaries, Indian learners used English education to question authority, access global ideas, and reinterpret their own cultural heritage. The classroom became a site of both influence and resistance.

Colonial education played a decisive role in reshaping Indian intellectual life by introducing Western systems of knowledge, modes of reasoning, and literary traditions. Through English education, Indian students encountered new disciplines such as modern science, political theory, philosophy, and English literature. These subjects emphasized rational inquiry, empirical thinking, and individual expression, which differed in form and method from many traditional modes of learning. As a result, English education did not merely transfer information but transformed the way knowledge itself was approached and understood.

From the colonial perspective, the purpose of English education was largely administrative. Policies influenced by figures such as Thomas Babington Macaulay aimed to create a class of educated Indians who could assist in governance by acting as intermediaries between the rulers and the wider population. English was promoted as a language of efficiency and modernity, while indigenous languages and knowledge systems were often sidelined. However, the outcomes of this educational project extended far beyond colonial intentions.

Indian learners actively appropriated English education to engage with global ideas of liberty, equality, nationalism, and social reform. Exposure to Western political thought encouraged critical reflection on colonial rule, social hierarchies, and inherited customs. Rather than accepting colonial authority uncritically, many students used the intellectual tools gained through English education to question domination and argue for self-respect, reform, and freedom. In this way, English became a language through which resistance and reform could be articulated.

At the same time, English education enabled Indians to reinterpret their own cultural and philosophical traditions. Educated thinkers began to reassess Indian history, religion, and literature using new critical frameworks, often defending indigenous values in modern terms. The colonial classroom thus emerged as a complex space-one of influence and control, but also of dialogue and dissent. It fostered an intellectual awakening in which English served not only as an instrument of colonial power, but also as a means for Indians to redefine identity, knowledge, and purpose in a changing world.

Example: Colonial Education as a Tool of Transformation and Resistance

A clear example of how colonial education led to intellectual transformation is seen in the work of Raja Ram Mohan Roy . Educated in both traditional Indian learning and English-based Western education, he used English not as a symbol of submission but as a medium for reform and critical dialogue. Through his exposure to Western philosophy, rationalism, and humanist ideas, he began questioning social practices such as sati and rigid religious orthodoxy.

Raja Ram Mohan Roy employed English education to reinterpret Indian cultural and religious texts, arguing that many regressive customs were distortions rather than authentic traditions. He wrote essays, petitions, and reformist arguments in English to communicate with colonial authorities as well as the global intellectual community. This strategic use of English allowed him to challenge colonial assumptions about Indian society while simultaneously advocating social reform within India.

This example shows how the colonial classroom became a space of both influence and resistance. While English education was introduced to serve colonial administration, Indian intellectuals like Raja Ram Mohan Roy transformed it into a tool for questioning authority, promoting reform, and redefining Indian identity in a modern, global context.

1.3 Indian Response to the English Language

Rather than passive adoption, Indians actively responded to English by adapting it to local contexts. Writers, thinkers, and reformers infused English with Indian themes, values, and concerns. This process marked the beginning of English as a medium through which Indian consciousness could be expressed without abandoning cultural roots.

The Indian response to the English language was marked by active engagement rather than passive acceptance. Instead of treating English solely as a foreign or imposed medium, Indians gradually adapted it to suit local realities, emotions, and intellectual needs. English was reshaped to express Indian social experiences, moral questions, spiritual ideas, and cultural identities. This adaptation reflected a conscious effort to use the language as a bridge between Indian traditions and global modernity.

Indian writers and thinkers began to infuse English with indigenous themes drawn from history, mythology, social life, and philosophical traditions. While the language itself was English, the content, imagery, and worldview were distinctly Indian. Early intellectuals such as **Bankim Chandra Chattopadhyay** and later **Rabindranath Tagore** demonstrated that English could be moulded to convey Indian sensibilities without erasing cultural roots. Their engagement showed that language could be appropriated and transformed rather than merely inherited.

This creative response also allowed Indians to speak back to colonial power. By using English to narrate Indian histories, critique social injustices, and articulate nationalist aspirations, writers challenged colonial stereotypes that portrayed Indian culture as inferior or stagnant. English thus became a medium for self-representation, enabling Indians to define themselves on their own terms in national and international spheres.

Over time, this process led to the emergence of Indian English as a distinct form of expression. It carried Indian rhythms of thought, cultural references, and ethical concerns, even while operating within the structure of the English language. The Indian response to English, therefore, marked a crucial intellectual shift: English was no longer just the language of rulers, but a powerful instrument through which Indian consciousness, identity, and cultural continuity could be expressed and preserved.

1.4 English as a Tool of Expression and Empowerment

Over time, English evolved from a colonial instrument into a platform for self-representation. Indian thinkers used it to voice social reform, national identity, and ethical inquiry. This transformation demonstrates how the Indian mind reshaped English to serve intellectual freedom and cultural articulation.

Over time, English in India underwent a significant transformation-from a language associated with colonial authority to a powerful medium of self-expression and empowerment. What was once introduced as an instrument of governance and control gradually became a platform through which Indians articulated their own voices, concerns, and aspirations. This shift reflected the ability of Indian thinkers to reinterpret English in ways that served intellectual independence rather than colonial dominance.

Indian reformers and writers used English to address pressing social issues such as inequality, gender injustice, caste discrimination, and moral reform.

By employing English, they were able to reach wider audiences, both within India and beyond, ensuring that Indian perspectives entered global debates. Thinkers like Mahatma Gandhi and Jawaharlal Nehru used English extensively to express ideas of ethical politics, national unity, and human dignity. Their writings demonstrate how English became a language of persuasion, dialogue, and conscience.

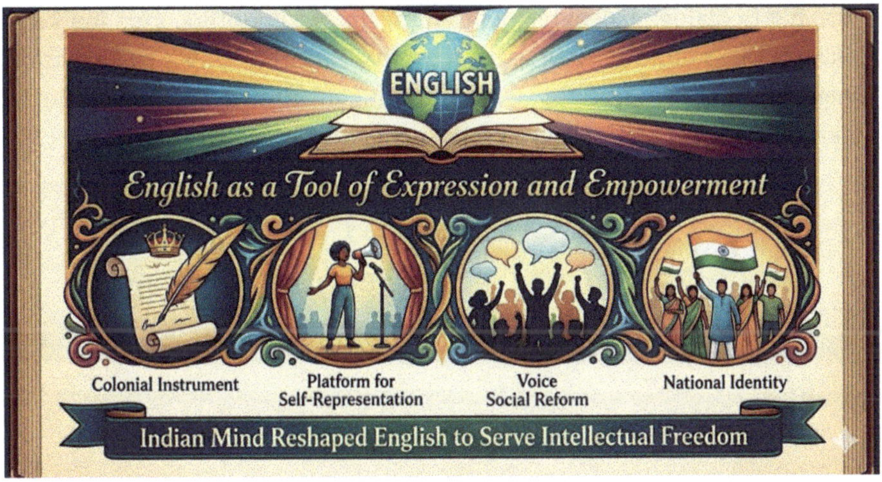

English also enabled the articulation of national identity during the freedom movement. Political speeches, essays, and philosophical reflections written in English allowed Indian leaders to challenge colonial narratives and present an alternative vision of India grounded in justice, pluralism, and self-rule. Through this process, English ceased to be merely a borrowed language and evolved into a means of asserting intellectual freedom and moral authority.

This transformation highlights the creative agency of the Indian mind. By reshaping English to convey indigenous values, historical experiences, and ethical concerns, Indians turned a colonial language into an instrument of cultural articulation and empowerment. English thus emerged not as a force that erased identity, but as a medium that enabled Indians to speak for themselves, engage with the world, and assert their place in global intellectual discourse. **1.5 Reclaiming Voice: Indian Thought in a Global Intellectual Landscape**

As English became a tool of expression and empowerment, it also enabled Indian thought to move beyond national boundaries and participate actively in global intellectual conversations. The adoption of English did not merely allow Indians to speak *to* the world; it allowed them to speak *with* the world, engaging in dialogue, debate, and critique on equal footing. This marked a crucial transition from intellectual marginalization to global participation, where Indian perspectives were no longer filtered through colonial interpretation but articulated directly by Indian voices themselves.

Indian thinkers used English to reinterpret indigenous philosophies, ethical systems, and cultural traditions for a global audience. Concepts rooted in Indian civilization—such as dharma, non-violence, spiritual pluralism, and collective responsibility—were expressed in a language that enabled cross-cultural understanding. Rather than diluting these ideas, English often served as a bridge that translated complex indigenous thought into globally accessible discourse. This process demonstrated that Indian intellectual traditions were not insular or antiquated but deeply relevant to universal questions about justice, morality, governance, and human purpose.

The global circulation of Indian ideas through English also challenged dominant Western assumptions about knowledge production. For centuries, intellectual authority had been concentrated in Eurocentric institutions and traditions. Indian scholars, writers, and reformers disrupted this imbalance by contributing alternative frameworks of understanding rooted in lived social realities, spiritual inquiry, and historical experience. Through essays, speeches, books, and international forums, Indian thinkers presented perspectives that questioned materialism, colonial hierarchies, and rigid rationalism, offering more holistic views of human development.

This reclaiming of voice was particularly significant in political and ethical discourse. Indian contributions to debates on freedom, civil rights, democracy, and peace reshaped global thinking during critical moments of the twentieth century. The articulation of non-violent resistance, ethical leadership, and inclusive nationalism resonated far beyond India's borders. These ideas influenced global movements for social justice and political reform, demonstrating that Indian intellectual contributions were not reactive or derivative but innovative and transformative.

English also enabled Indian scholars to engage with modern scientific, legal, and philosophical developments without abandoning cultural roots. Rather than viewing tradition and modernity as opposing forces, Indian thinkers often framed them as complementary. Ancient texts, oral traditions, and ethical teachings were re-examined through modern analytical lenses, creating a synthesis that enriched both indigenous knowledge and contemporary scholarship. This integrative approach allowed Indian thought to evolve dynamically while maintaining continuity with its philosophical heritage.

The global academic space further expanded opportunities for Indian voices to shape disciplines such as philosophy, sociology, literature, political theory, and education. Indian scholars writing in English contributed to redefining these fields by introducing themes of colonial experience, postcolonial identity, cultural hybridity, and ethical pluralism. Their work challenged simplistic narratives and emphasized complexity, diversity, and historical context. In doing so, Indian intellectuals helped broaden the scope of global scholarship, making it more inclusive and representative.

At the cultural level, English became a medium through which Indian identity was asserted rather than erased. Writers used it to explore questions of belonging, displacement, tradition, and change, capturing the nuanced realities of a society navigating continuity and transformation. These narratives resisted homogenization and presented India as a pluralistic, evolving civilization rather than a static cultural artifact. By expressing these realities in English, Indian voices reached international audiences without compromising authenticity.

Importantly, the use of English did not replace indigenous languages or knowledge systems but existed alongside them. For many Indian thinkers, multilingualism became a strength rather than a limitation. Ideas circulated across languages, enriching public discourse and strengthening intellectual exchange within India and beyond. English functioned as one strand in a broader linguistic and cultural ecosystem, enabling dialogue across regions, communities, and nations.

The empowerment derived from this global engagement lay in the ability to define oneself rather than be defined by others. Indian thinkers no longer depended on external validation to assert intellectual legitimacy. By contributing original ideas, critiques, and frameworks, they demonstrated intellectual self-confidence and cultural agency. This shift altered how India was perceived globally—not merely as a subject of study but as a producer of knowledge and thought.

In contemporary times, this legacy continues to shape education, research, and public discourse. Indian scholars, educators, and writers actively participate in global conversations on technology, ethics, sustainability, and governance. Their contributions reflect a confidence rooted in historical experience and philosophical depth. The foundations laid by earlier generations of thinkers ensured that English would remain a tool not of dependency but of dialogue, negotiation, and influence.

Ultimately, reclaiming voice in a global intellectual landscape represents the culmination of the transformation described in earlier sections. English, once imposed, was reshaped to carry Indian thought across borders without severing cultural roots. This process affirmed that empowerment lies not in rejecting external influences outright, but in appropriating them creatively and purposefully. By doing so, the Indian mind asserted its presence in global discourse—confident, critical, and deeply grounded in its own intellectual traditions.

Multiple Choice Questions (MCQs)

1. The English language first entered the Indian subcontinent primarily through:

A. Missionary activities

B. Trade and commerce

C. Literary exchange

D. Cultural migration

Answer: B. Trade and commerce

2. Which organization played a central role in introducing English for administrative purposes in India?

A. Indian National Congress

B. British Parliament

C. British East India Company

D. Royal Asiatic Society

Answer: C. British East India Company

3. In its early phase, English in India was mainly used as a language of:

A. Creative literature

B. Religious instruction

C. Governance and administration

D. Popular entertainment

Answer: C. Governance and administration

4. Colonial education policies primarily aimed to:

A. Promote Indian culture globally

B. Eliminate indigenous languages

C. Create administrative intermediaries

D. Encourage mass literacy

Answer: C. Create administrative intermediaries

5. English education introduced Indians to which of the following most directly?

A. Only British customs

B. Western philosophy, science, and literature

C. Regional folklore

D. Oral traditions

Answer: B. Western philosophy, science, and literature

Short Answer Questions

1. What circumstances led to the introduction of English in India?
2. How did colonial education influence Indian intellectual life?
3. Why was English associated with power during British rule?
4. What role did English play in social reform movements?
5. How did Indians respond creatively to the English language?
6. In what way did English move beyond administration into culture?

Long Answer Questions

1. Trace the historical journey of English in India.
2. Discuss the impact of colonial education on Indian consciousness.
3. Analyse English as both an instrument of control and empowerment.
4. Examine how Indians transformed English into a medium of expression.
5. Evaluate the role of English in shaping modern Indian thought.

2

Language, Identity, and Cultural Negotiation

2.1 Language as a Marker of Identity

Language plays a crucial role in shaping personal and collective identity. For Indian writers, English became a means to negotiate who they were in a society shaped by tradition, modernity, and colonial experience. Writing in English allowed them to define identity beyond rigid regional or linguistic boundaries.

Language is far more than a tool of communication; it functions as a powerful marker of identity, shaping how individuals and communities perceive themselves and are perceived by others. In the Indian context, identity has traditionally been linked to region, religion, caste, and mother tongue. However, the introduction and later adoption of English added a new dimension to this identity formation. For Indian writers, English did not merely replace indigenous languages; instead, it became a medium through which complex layers of selfhood could be expressed and reinterpreted.

The use of English enabled Indian writers to articulate identities that were not confined to a single region or linguistic tradition. Writing in a language that was not tied to one specific Indian community allowed authors to transcend local boundaries and address a broader, often global, audience. This helped shape a more inclusive sense of identity-one that could simultaneously acknowledge Indian cultural roots while engaging with modern, cosmopolitan ideas. English thus acted as a bridge between inherited traditions and emerging modern sensibilities.

At the same time, English carried the weight of colonial history, making its use both challenging and transformative. Indian writers reshaped the language by infusing it with indigenous idioms, cultural references, and local rhythms of speech. This process turned English into a uniquely Indian expressive form, reflecting lived realities rather than colonial authority. Through this adaptation, writers asserted ownership over the language and used it to voice their experiences, aspirations, and struggles.

Ultimately, language as a marker of identity in Indian English writing represents negotiation rather than replacement. English became a space where Indian writers could explore hybrid identities-rooted in tradition yet open to change. By redefining the language to suit their cultural context, they demonstrated that identity is dynamic and evolving, shaped not only by heritage but also by historical experience and creative expression.

Aspect	Role of Language	Impact on Identity
Personal Identity	Language shapes self-expression and thought patterns	Writers use English to articulate individual experiences beyond regional limits
Collective Identity	Language connects communities and shared experiences	English enables a pan-Indian identity not restricted to one native language
Cultural Negotiation	Language reflects interaction between tradition and modernity	Indian writers blend cultural values with contemporary ideas through English
Colonial Legacy	English carries historical and political significance	Writers reclaim and reshape English to assert postcolonial identity
Literary Expression	Language serves as a creative medium	Indianized English reflects local realities, idioms, and social concerns

Global Engagement	Language determines audience reach	English allows Indian writers to participate in global literary discourse

2.2 Cultural Hybridity and Dual Belonging

Indian English literature reflects a hybrid consciousness where indigenous cultural values coexist with global influences. Writers navigate between inherited traditions and contemporary realities, creating texts that reflect cultural negotiation rather than cultural loss. This hybridity becomes a defining feature of Indian literary expression in English.

Cultural hybridity is a defining characteristic of Indian English literature, emerging from the interaction between indigenous traditions and global influences. Indian writers writing in English often inhabit a space of dual belonging-rooted in local cultural practices while simultaneously engaging with modern, international ideas. This duality does not suggest confusion or conflict; rather, it reflects a lived reality shaped by history, education, migration, and cross-cultural contact. As a result, Indian English literature becomes a site where multiple cultural influences coexist and interact meaningfully.

In these literary works, traditional elements such as family values, rituals, mythology, and social customs frequently appear alongside themes of urbanization, individualism, gender equality, and global mobility. Writers portray characters who negotiate between the expectations of their cultural heritage and the demands of contemporary life. This negotiation is not presented as a rejection of tradition but as an adaptive process through which culture evolves. The coexistence of the old and the new highlights the flexibility and resilience of Indian culture rather than its erosion.

The use of English further intensifies this hybrid consciousness. Although English originated as a colonial language, Indian writers transform it by embedding local expressions, cultural symbols, and Indian modes of thinking. This results in a distinct literary voice that reflects both local specificity and global awareness. Through this process, English becomes a tool for expressing cultural complexity rather than a marker of cultural displacement.

Ultimately, cultural hybridity in Indian English literature represents creative synthesis rather than cultural loss. The sense of dual belonging allows writers to articulate identities that are layered, dynamic, and inclusive. By embracing hybridity, Indian English literature presents culture as fluid and evolving, capturing the realities of a society shaped by both tradition and change.

2.3 Tension Between Native Languages and English

The use of English has often raised concerns about cultural displacement. This section examines the tension between English and Indian languages, showing how writers balance respect for mother tongues while using English as a wider communicative tool. Many texts reveal a conscious effort to preserve cultural authenticity within an English framework.

The use of English in Indian literature has long generated a sense of tension between native languages and a foreign medium of expression. Indian languages such as Hindi, Bengali, Tamil, Urdu, and others are deeply tied to regional culture, emotional expression, and collective memory. The adoption of English, therefore, often raises concerns about cultural displacement, linguistic loss, and the marginalization of mother tongues. This tension is not merely linguistic but cultural, as language carries values, worldviews, and historical continuity.

Indian English writers are acutely aware of this dilemma and frequently address it within their works. Rather than abandoning native languages, many writers treat English as an additional communicative tool rather than a replacement. English enables wider national and global reach, but the emotional and cultural depth of indigenous languages continues to shape thought, dialogue, and narrative sensibility. As a result, Indian English literature often reflects an internal struggle between intimacy with the mother tongue and the practicality of English.

To balance this tension, writers consciously preserve cultural authenticity within an English framework. Native words, phrases, idioms, and untranslatable expressions are often retained to convey cultural nuance. Code-switching, untranslated terms, and culturally specific metaphors allow writers to maintain the presence of Indian languages within English texts. This strategy asserts the continued relevance of mother tongues while adapting English to Indian realities.

Ultimately, the tension between native languages and English becomes a creative force rather than a limitation. Indian English literature demonstrates that respect for linguistic heritage can coexist with the use of a global language. By reshaping English to accommodate indigenous cultural expression, writers ensure that their literary works remain rooted in Indian sensibilities while participating in broader literary conversations.

2.4 English as an Indianized Language

Indian writers reshape English by incorporating local idioms, rhythms, and cultural references. This process of Indianization demonstrates that English is no longer an external language but one that reflects Indian thought patterns. The result is a distinct linguistic identity rooted in Indian experience.

English in Indian literary writing has undergone a significant transformation, evolving from a colonial language into a medium deeply rooted in Indian experience. Indian writers do not use English in its original, standardized British form; instead, they reshape it by incorporating local idioms, speech patterns, cultural references, and indigenous ways of thinking. This process of Indianization reflects a conscious effort to make the language expressive of Indian realities rather than foreign sensibilities.

Dimension	Indianization of English	Resulting Linguistic Identity
Vocabulary	Use of Indian words, kinship terms, cultural objects, and emotions	Preserves cultural meanings that lack direct English equivalents
Sentence Structure	Influence of Indian language syntax and speech rhythms	Creates a distinctive flow reflecting Indian modes of expression
Idioms and Expressions	Inclusion of local idioms, proverbs, and colloquial phrases	Enhances authenticity and cultural rootedness
Cultural References	Depiction of Indian customs, rituals, festivals, and social systems	Grounds English narratives in Indian lived experience
Thought Patterns	Reflection of Indian storytelling traditions and emotional intensity	Aligns language with Indian cognitive and narrative styles
Ownership of Language	English adapted rather than imitated	Establishes English as an Indian expressive medium

One of the most visible features of Indianized English is the inclusion of native words, phrases, and expressions that remain untranslated. Terms related to relationships, rituals, food, emotions, and social customs are often retained because they carry meanings that English equivalents cannot fully convey. Along with vocabulary, sentence structures influenced by Indian languages give the prose a distinctive rhythm. This stylistic adaptation allows writers to preserve cultural nuance while communicating through English.

Indian writers also embed cultural contexts such as joint family systems, social hierarchies, religious diversity, festivals, and everyday practices into English narratives. As a result, English begins to mirror Indian thought patterns-circular reasoning, oral storytelling traditions, emotional intensity, and symbolic imagery. The language becomes flexible enough to accommodate Indian sensibilities without losing clarity or depth.

Through this creative transformation, English is no longer perceived as an external or imposed language. It becomes an Indian language in expression, ownership, and identity. The Indianization of English establishes a distinct linguistic identity that reflects the lived experiences of Indian society,

demonstrating that language evolves through use and cultural adaptation. Indian English literature thus stands as evidence that English, when reshaped creatively, can authentically represent indigenous voices and cultural consciousness.

Multiple Choice Questions (MCQ)

1. In Indian English literature, language primarily functions as

A. A tool of entertainment

B. A marker of identity

C. A replacement for Indian languages

D. A purely colonial influence   Answer: B

2. Writing in English helped Indian writers to

A. Reject indigenous cultures

B. Confine identity to regional boundaries

C. Express identity beyond linguistic and regional limits

D. Avoid social issues Answer: C

3. Cultural hybridity in Indian English literature refers to

A. Complete Westernization

B. Loss of traditional values

C. Coexistence of indigenous and global influences

D. Rejection of English language Answer: C

4. Dual belonging in Indian English literature means

A. Loyalty to two foreign cultures

B. Conflict between tradition and modernity

C. Simultaneous connection to local culture and global ideas

D. Cultural confusion Answer: C

5. The tension between native languages and English mainly arises due to

A. Difficulty in grammar

B. Fear of cultural displacement

C. Limited readership

D. Literary competition Answer: B

Short Answer Questions

1. How does language contribute to identity formation?

2. What is meant by cultural negotiation?

3. Define cultural hybridity.

4. Why is English both inclusive and exclusive in India?

5. What tension exists between English and native languages?

6. What is meant by the Indianization of English?

Long Answer Questions

1. Discuss the relationship between language and identity in Indian English literature.

2. Analyse cultural hybridity as reflected in Indian English writing.

3. Examine the role of English in negotiating tradition and modernity.

4. Is English a threat to Indian languages? Critically evaluate.

5. Explain how Indian writers adapt English to local contexts.

6. Discuss English as a space of cultural negotiation in India.

3

Indian Sensibility in English Prose

3.1 Narrative Style and Indian Storytelling Traditions

Indian prose in English often reflects oral storytelling traditions, layered narratives, and moral reflection. Unlike linear Western narration, Indian prose may emphasize memory, reflection, and cyclical time. These stylistic choices reveal how Indian sensibility influences narrative structure.

Indian prose written in English often carries deep imprints of indigenous storytelling traditions that long predate the written word. Indian storytelling has historically evolved through oral forms such as folktales, epics, myths, parables, and devotional narratives. When Indian writers adopt English as a medium, they do not abandon these traditions; instead, they **rework English prose to accommodate Indian narrative sensibilities** .

One of the most distinctive features of Indian storytelling is its **oral influence**. Stories are often told as if they are being spoken rather than formally written, creating a conversational tone that draws the reader into the narrative. This oral quality allows for digressions, repetitions, anecdotes, and reflective pauses, which differ from the tightly structured, plot-driven narration commonly associated with Western prose. Such storytelling mirrors the way stories are shared within families, communities, and cultural gatherings in India.

Another key element is the use of **layered and non-linear narratives** . Indian prose frequently moves back and forth between past and present, blending memories, myths, and personal experiences. Time is often treated as **cyclical rather than strictly linear** , reflecting Indian philosophical ideas where past, present, and future coexist. This narrative approach allows writers to explore history, identity, and memory simultaneously rather than following a straight chronological sequence.

Indian storytelling also places strong emphasis on **moral reflection and philosophical insight** . Narratives are not merely meant to entertain but to provoke thought, convey ethical dilemmas, and reflect on human values. Writers often embed social commentary, cultural wisdom, and spiritual questioning within the story, echoing the didactic nature of traditional Indian tales.

Through these stylistic choices-oral tone, non-linear structure, reflective depth, and moral consciousness-Indian prose in English reshapes the language itself. The result is a narrative style that clearly reflects **Indian cultural consciousness** , demonstrating that English, when used by Indian writers, becomes a powerful medium for expressing indigenous storytelling traditions rather than replacing them.

3.2 Social Reality and Everyday Life

Indian English prose frequently focuses on social realities such as caste, class, family, and community life. Writers use English to depict local environments with emotional depth and realism. This grounding in lived experience ensures that the prose remains culturally rooted despite the foreign medium.

Indian English prose is deeply anchored in the **social realities of everyday life**, making it a powerful medium for representing lived experiences across diverse Indian contexts. Rather than focusing on abstract themes alone, Indian writers frequently engage with concrete social structures such as **caste hierarchies, class divisions, family relationships, gender roles, and community dynamics**. These elements form the backbone of many narratives, ensuring that the prose remains socially relevant and culturally authentic.

Social Reality and Everyday Life -

One significant feature of Indian English prose is its **attention to ordinary lives**. Writers often portray the daily routines, struggles, aspirations, and conflicts of common people-teachers, farmers, clerks, housewives, students, and labourers. By focusing on everyday settings such as homes, villages, streets, markets, and workplaces, authors present a realistic picture of Indian society as it is experienced from within, rather than as an outsider's observation.

Family and community play a central role in shaping individual identity in Indian society, and this is clearly reflected in prose narratives. Indian English writers explore **intergenerational relationships, traditions, expectations, and emotional bonds**, highlighting how personal choices are influenced by collective values. Conflicts between tradition and modernity, duty and desire, or individual freedom and social responsibility often emerge from these close-knit social structures.

Issues of **caste and class** are also treated with sensitivity and depth. Writers use English as a tool to expose social inequalities, discrimination, and power dynamics while giving voice to marginalized experiences. At the same time, the language is adapted to convey local speech patterns, cultural references, and emotional nuances, preventing the narrative from feeling detached or artificial.

Through realistic settings, emotionally grounded characters, and socially conscious themes, Indian English prose successfully captures the **texture of everyday Indian life**. Although English may be a borrowed language, its use becomes naturalized through lived experience, ensuring that the writing remains firmly rooted in Indian culture and social reality.

Examples of Social Reality and Everyday Life in Indian English Prose

Indian English prose offers rich and authentic portrayals of everyday social life by grounding narratives in lived experience. The following examples clearly illustrate how writers depict social realities such as caste, class, family, and community while writing in English.

1. *Untouchable*

This novel presents a single day in the life of Bakha, a young boy belonging to a marginalized caste. Through ordinary events-cleaning streets, visiting the marketplace, interacting with upper-caste individuals-the narrative exposes the harsh realities of caste discrimination. The prose focuses on routine social interactions to highlight systemic inequality, showing how everyday life itself becomes a site of oppression. English is used not to distance the experience but to amplify the emotional and social truth of lived reality.

2. *Malgudi Days*

Set in the fictional town of Malgudi, this work captures middle-class Indian life through simple, relatable characters such as shopkeepers, teachers, and schoolchildren. The stories depict family bonds, social customs, small ambitions, and moral dilemmas rooted in daily life. Narayan's understated prose reflects Indian rhythms of speech and thought, demonstrating how English can naturally express local culture without losing authenticity.

3. *The White Tiger*

This novel portrays the sharp divide between rural poverty and urban wealth in contemporary India. Through the personal journey of its narrator, the narrative explores class struggle, social mobility, and survival within everyday social systems. The use of English is direct and conversational, reflecting the lived experiences of individuals navigating inequality in modern Indian society.

3.3 Ethical and Philosophical Concerns

Indian prose writing often carries a strong ethical dimension, addressing questions of duty, justice, and human relationships. Influenced by Indian philosophical traditions, writers use prose to explore moral dilemmas and inner conflicts, blending introspection with social commentary.

Indian prose writing in English is marked by a **strong ethical and philosophical orientation**, reflecting the deep influence of India's intellectual and spiritual traditions. Rather than treating morality as an abstract concept, Indian writers embed ethical questions within everyday situations, personal relationships, and social structures. This approach allows prose narratives to function as spaces for **moral inquiry and self-examination**, not merely as storytelling devices.

A central concern in Indian prose is the idea of **duty and responsibility**. Characters are often placed in situations where personal desires conflict with social obligations-to family, community, or society at large. These tensions reflect long-standing Indian philosophical ideas that emphasize moral responsibility, balance, and conscious action. Writers explore how individuals negotiate these demands, revealing the psychological and emotional cost of ethical choices.

Indian prose also frequently addresses **justice and social ethics**. Questions of fairness, inequality, compassion, and moral accountability appear through narratives dealing with caste, gender, poverty, and power. Instead of offering simple solutions, writers present ethical dilemmas in their complexity, encouraging readers to reflect on the structures that shape moral behaviour. In this way, prose becomes a medium for social critique grounded in ethical reflection.

Another defining feature is the emphasis on **inner conflict and introspection**. Indian writers often delve deeply into the inner lives of their characters, portraying moments of doubt, guilt, realization, and moral awakening. This inward focus aligns with Indian philosophical traditions that value self-knowledge and reflection as paths to ethical understanding. The narrative voice frequently pauses to contemplate motives, consequences, and moral implications, blending storytelling with philosophical meditation.

By combining **introspection with social commentary**, Indian prose writing transforms English into a vehicle for ethical exploration rooted in Indian thought. The result is literature that not only portrays society but also questions how individuals should live within it, making ethical and philosophical concerns a defining strength of Indian English prose.

Ethical / Philosophical Aspect	Description	Reflection in Prose Narratives	Cultural Significance
Duty and Responsibility	Focus on moral obligations toward family, society, and self	Characters face conflicts between personal desire and social duty	Reflects Indian emphasis on responsibility and ethical conduct
Justice and Social Ethics	Engagement with fairness, inequality, and moral accountability	Narratives highlight caste, class, gender, and power dynamics	Encourages ethical awareness and social reform
Inner Conflict and Introspection	Exploration of moral doubt, guilt, and self-questioning	Writers depict characters' inner struggles and ethical dilemmas	Aligns with Indian philosophical focus on self-realization
Moral Dilemmas	Situations with no easy ethical choices	Prose presents complex decisions without clear right or wrong	Promotes reflective and critical thinking
Compassion and Human Values	Emphasis on empathy, kindness, and human relationships	Stories foreground emotional bonds and moral sensitivity	Reinforces humanistic and spiritual traditions

Blending Philosophy with Social Life	Ethical ideas integrated into everyday situations	Moral reflection emerges from ordinary experiences	Makes philosophy accessible and lived rather than abstract

3.4 Prose as a Medium of Cultural Reflection

Through essays, novels, and short stories, Indian writers turn English prose into a mirror of society. The language becomes a space where cultural change, continuity, and conflict are examined. Indian sensibility transforms prose into a reflective tool rather than mere narrative expression.

Indian English prose functions not merely as a narrative form but as a reflective medium through which society examines itself . Through essays, novels, and short stories, Indian writers use prose to observe, question, and reinterpret cultural realities. English, though originally a colonial language, is reshaped to express Indian experiences, values, and contradictions, turning prose into a mirror of social life rather than a neutral storytelling tool.

One important role of prose is its ability to capture cultural change and continuity. Indian society is marked by constant negotiation between tradition and modernity-between inherited customs and evolving social norms. Prose writing records this transition by portraying changing family structures, shifting gender roles, urbanization, education, and globalization, while also preserving cultural memory, rituals, and collective beliefs. In this way, prose documents both what is transforming and what endures.

Indian English prose also becomes a space to explore cultural conflict and tension. Writers examine clashes between generations, rural and urban values, faith and rationality, individual freedom and social expectations. These conflicts are not presented as isolated problems but as part of a larger cultural dialogue. By situating personal stories within broader social frameworks, prose highlights how individual lives are shaped by cultural forces.

Essays and reflective prose further deepen this cultural role by offering **critical commentary and self-examination** . Writers often adopt a contemplative tone, questioning social practices, moral assumptions, and collective identities. This reflective quality allows prose to move beyond description toward interpretation, encouraging readers to think critically about their society.

Through these functions, Indian sensibility transforms English prose into a **tool of cultural reflection** . It becomes a language of observation, critique, and introspection-one that not only tells stories but also helps society understand itself.

Aspect	Core Focus	Narrative / Stylistic Features	Cultural Significance
3.1 Narrative Style and Indian Storytelling Traditions	Influence of indigenous storytelling forms	Oral tone, layered narratives, non-linear structure, cyclical sense of time, moral reflection	Reflects Indian ways of remembering, narrating, and understanding life beyond linear Western models
3.2 Social Reality and Everyday Life	Representation of lived social experience	Realistic depiction of caste, class, family, and community; emotionally grounded settings	Ensures cultural rootedness and authenticity despite the use of English

3.3 Ethical and Philosophical Concerns	Moral and philosophical inquiry	Exploration of duty, justice, relationships, inner conflict, and self-reflection	Draws from Indian philosophical traditions and promotes ethical awareness
3.4 Prose as a Medium of Cultural Reflection	Society as a subject of examination	Essays, novels, and short stories used for critique, reflection, and interpretation	Transforms English prose into a mirror of cultural change, continuity, and conflict

Multiple Choice Questions (MCQs)

1. Indian prose in English often reflects which traditional mode of storytelling?

   a) Scientific narration

   b) Oral storytelling tradition

   c) Journalistic reporting

   d) Technical documentation

Answer: b) Oral storytelling tradition

2. Which concept of time is commonly emphasized in Indian English prose?

   a) Strictly linear time

   b) Mechanical time

c) Cyclical time

d) Future-oriented time

Answer: c) Cyclical time

3. Indian English prose differs from Western narration mainly in its focus on:

a) Fast-paced action

b) Fantasy elements

c) Memory and reflection

d) Scientific realism

Answer: c) Memory and reflection

4. Which social realities are frequently depicted in Indian English prose?

a) Only urban elite lifestyles

b) Global corporate culture

c) Caste, class, family, and community life

d) Mythical societies

Answer: c) Caste, class, family, and community life

5. The use of English by Indian writers primarily serves to:

a) Imitate Western culture

b) Replace Indian languages

c) Express Indian lived experiences

d) Promote colonial values

Answer: c) Express Indian lived experiences

Short Answer Questions

1. What features distinguish Indian English prose?
2. How does social reality shape Indian prose writing?
3. What role does morality play in Indian English fiction?
4. Why is realism important in Indian English prose?
5. How does prose reflect Indian storytelling traditions?
6. What themes recur in Indian English novels?

Long Answer Questions

1. Discuss how Indian sensibility influences English prose writing.
2. Analyse the portrayal of social issues in Indian English fiction.
3. Examine ethical and philosophical concerns in Indian English prose.
4. How does Indian prose adapt Western narrative forms?
5. Prose acts as a mirror of Indian society-discuss.
6. Evaluate Indian English prose as a cultural document.

4

Poetry in English and the Indian Inner World

4.1 Indian Imagery and Symbolism in English Poetry

Indian poets writing in English frequently draw upon indigenous imagery such as rivers, seasons, rituals, festivals, and sacred spaces. These symbols carry emotional, cultural, and spiritual meanings rooted in Indian life.

Indian English poetry is deeply enriched by imagery and symbolism drawn from the lived cultural, spiritual, and natural environment of India. Poets writing in English often turn to familiar elements such as rivers, seasons, festivals, rituals, village landscapes, temples, and everyday domestic scenes. These images are not used merely for decoration; they carry layered meanings shaped by centuries of collective memory and cultural practice.

Through such symbolism, Indian poets adapt the English language to express an inner world rooted in Indian thought and experience.

Natural imagery occupies a central place in Indian English poetry. Rivers like the Ganga or Yamuna, monsoons, scorching summers, and fertile harvest seasons are frequently evoked to reflect emotional states and philosophical ideas. For instance, the cyclical rhythm of seasons often symbolizes continuity, renewal, and the passage of time-concepts deeply embedded in Indian worldviews. When a poet describes the arrival of monsoon rains, it may simultaneously suggest relief, hope, spiritual cleansing, and emotional rebirth. In this way, nature becomes a symbolic language through which poets communicate both personal and collective meanings.

Religious and spiritual symbols also play a significant role. Temples, prayer lamps, incense, sacred chants, and mythological references appear frequently in Indian English poetry. These symbols reflect India's spiritual diversity and ethical traditions rather than promoting any single belief system. A simple image such as a flickering lamp may symbolize faith, inner awakening, or the fragile yet persistent nature of human hope. By using such imagery in English, poets transform a global language into a vessel for indigenous spiritual sensibilities.

Social and cultural imagery further strengthens this symbolic framework. Festivals like Diwali, Holi, or village fairs are often depicted to represent community life, shared joy, or social contrasts. Rituals surrounding birth, marriage, and death provide powerful symbolic material, allowing poets to explore themes of continuity, loss, and human relationships. These images ground poetry in everyday Indian life while elevating ordinary experiences into universal reflections.

Through the use of Indian imagery and symbolism, poets writing in English successfully bridge the gap between an inherited cultural identity and an adopted linguistic medium. English becomes more than a foreign language; it is reshaped to echo Indian emotions, philosophies, and social realities. As a result, Indian English poetry speaks both locally and globally, offering readers insight into the Indian inner world while engaging with universal human concerns.

4.2 Spirituality, Philosophy, and Emotional Depth

Indian English poetry often reflects spiritual inquiry and philosophical reflection. Influenced by Indian thought systems, poets explore themes such as selfhood, impermanence, devotion, and inner conflict. English becomes a flexible medium to articulate introspective journeys, blending rational expression with metaphysical depth characteristic of Indian consciousness.

Indian English poetry is deeply marked by spiritual inquiry and philosophical reflection, drawing inspiration from India's long traditions of introspection and metaphysical thought. Rather than focusing only on external events or material realities, many poets turn inward to examine the nature of the self, the meaning of existence, and the relationship between the individual and the larger universe. This inward gaze gives Indian English poetry a reflective tone in which emotion, thought, and spiritual questioning are closely intertwined.

A recurring theme in such poetry is the search for selfhood. Poets often explore questions like *Who am I?*, *What is the purpose of life?*, and *How does one reconcile desire with detachment?* These concerns reflect philosophical ideas common in Indian traditions, where self-realization is seen as a lifelong journey rather than a fixed achievement. English, in this context, becomes a tool for articulating subtle inner conflicts-between duty and desire, faith and doubt, action and withdrawal.

The idea of impermanence also occupies an important place. Indian English poets frequently reflect on the transient nature of life, relationships, and worldly success. Images of fading moments, passing seasons, or decaying bodies are used to express the fragility of human existence. However, this awareness of impermanence is often balanced with emotional acceptance rather than despair. Poetry thus becomes a space where loss, aging, and death are contemplated with calm reflection, emotional maturity, and philosophical depth.

Devotion and spirituality further enrich the emotional texture of Indian English poetry. Poets may express devotion not only to a divine presence but also to humanity, nature, or truth itself. Spiritual experience is often portrayed as deeply personal rather than ritualistic, focusing on inner awakening instead of outward religious practice. This allows poets to merge emotional sensitivity with spiritual insight, creating verses that resonate with quiet intensity rather than dramatic expression.

Overall, Indian English poetry transforms English into a flexible medium capable of expressing complex emotional and philosophical experiences. Rational language is infused with metaphysical depth, allowing poets to communicate the distinctive blend of spirituality, reflection, and emotional restraint that characterizes Indian consciousness. Through this synthesis, Indian English poetry speaks to universal human concerns while remaining rooted in a uniquely Indian way of understanding life and the self.

Example 1: Sri Aurobindo

Sri Aurobindo's poetry reflects deep spiritual inquiry rooted in Indian philosophy. His poems often explore the evolution of human consciousness and the soul's journey toward higher truth. Instead of focusing on personal emotions alone, he presents spirituality as a universal process of inner awakening. English is used as a philosophical medium to express ideas traditionally associated with Indian metaphysical thought, such as self-realization and unity between the individual and the cosmic force.

Relevance:
This example shows how Indian spirituality reshapes English poetry into a tool for philosophical reflection rather than mere emotional expression.

Example 2: Rabindranath Tagore

In Tagore's English poems, spirituality is closely linked with emotional depth and humanism. His poetry often portrays a personal dialogue between the self and the divine, where devotion is gentle, reflective, and inward. Rather than ritualistic religion, his poems emphasize love, surrender, and harmony with nature. Emotional sensitivity blends seamlessly with philosophical calm, giving the poems a meditative quality.

Relevance:
This demonstrates how devotion and emotional introspection coexist in Indian English poetry.

Example 3: Nissim Ezekiel

Nissim Ezekiel's poetry presents inner conflict and self-examination from a modern perspective. His poems often reflect doubts, moral questioning, and the struggle to find meaning in contemporary life. While his language is simple and rational, the themes reveal philosophical depth, especially concerning identity and faith. The tension between belief and scepticism highlights emotional honesty rather than blind devotion.

Relevance:
This example shows how Indian philosophy adapts to modern emotional realities through English.

4.3 Blending Traditional Sensibility with Modern Form

While using Western poetic forms such as free verse and sonnets, Indian poets retain a distinctly Indian sensibility. Rhythm, repetition, and reflective pauses echo classical Indian aesthetics.

Indian English poetry is distinguished by its ability to combine modern Western poetic forms with a deeply rooted Indian sensibility. While many Indian poets adopt structures such as free verse, blank verse, or even the sonnet-forms inherited from English literary traditions-they do not merely imitate Western models. Instead, they reshape these forms to express Indian ways of feeling, thinking, and perceiving reality. The result is a poetic style that is modern in structure but traditional in spirit.

One of the most noticeable features of this blending is the use of rhythm and repetition. Even in free verse, Indian poets often employ cyclical rhythms, recurring images, and reflective pauses that resemble patterns found in classical Indian poetry and oral traditions. These techniques echo the musicality of bhajans, folk songs, and classical verse, where repetition reinforces meaning and emotional intensity. Such rhythmic movement gives Indian English poetry a meditative and contemplative quality, distinguishing it from purely Western free verse.

Indian sensibility also emerges through reflective pauses and inward movement within the poem. Rather than driving the poem toward a sharp conclusion, poets often allow thoughts to unfold gradually, mirroring the Indian aesthetic preference for contemplation over urgency. Silence, pauses, and understatement become meaningful devices, suggesting emotional depth without overt dramatic expression. This approach reflects traditional Indian artistic values that emphasize suggestion and inner resonance rather than direct statement.

At the same time, Indian poets address contemporary themes such as urban life, identity conflicts, displacement, and social change. Modern experiences are expressed through modern forms, but they are interpreted through an

Indian cultural lens. Everyday moments-walking through a crowded street, observing rituals in a modern city, or reflecting on personal alienation-are

infused with cultural memory and philosophical reflection. This balance allows poets to remain relevant to present realities while staying connected to inherited traditions.

Overall, the blending of traditional sensibility with modern form demonstrates the creative adaptability of Indian English poetry. English poetic structures are not seen as restrictive frameworks but as flexible tools that can accommodate Indian rhythms, values, and emotional patterns. Through this fusion, Indian poets create a distinctive poetic voice-one that honours tradition while confidently engaging with modern literary expression.

4.4 Poetry as a Voice of Personal and Collective Identity

Poetry in English allows Indian writers to express personal emotions alongside collective memory. Themes of belonging, loss, cultural pride, and historical awareness surface through poetic expression. The poet's inner voice becomes a reflection of broader social and cultural realities, transforming individual emotion into shared consciousness.

Indian English poetry serves as a powerful medium through which poets express both individual emotions and shared cultural experiences. While poetry often begins with personal feelings-such as longing, nostalgia, pride, or grief-it frequently expands beyond the private self to reflect collective memory and social identity. In the Indian context, the personal and the collective are closely connected, and poetry becomes a space where individual voice naturally merges with community consciousness.

Themes of belonging and identity are central to this poetic expression. Indian poets writing in English often reflect on questions of roots, homeland, and cultural inheritance. Feelings of attachment to land, language, family, and tradition appear alongside experiences of migration, urbanization, or cultural displacement. Through poetry, writers negotiate who they are in relation to their society, history, and changing world. Personal memories thus become symbols of a larger cultural experience shared by many.

Collective memory also plays a significant role in shaping poetic identity. References to historical events, colonial experience, freedom struggles, social reform, or traditional customs allow poets to connect their inner emotions with the past of the nation or community. Even when a poem speaks in an individual tone, it often carries echoes of shared struggles and aspirations. In this way, poetry preserves cultural memory while interpreting it through a contemporary and personal lens.

Poetry in English further allows Indian writers to express cultural pride and social awareness. By writing about indigenous traditions, social realities, and ethical concerns in a global language, poets assert the value of Indian identity on an international platform. English becomes a medium not of cultural loss, but of cultural assertion. The poet's voice represents both self-expression and cultural representation, giving dignity and visibility to Indian experiences.

Ultimately, Indian English poetry transforms personal emotion into shared consciousness. The poet's inner reflections resonate with collective feelings, making poetry a bridge between the self and society. Through this fusion, poetry becomes not only a literary form but also a voice of identity-one that captures the emotional, cultural, and historical essence of Indian life while speaking to universal human concerns.

Multiple Choice Questions (MCQs)

1. Indian English poetry primarily reflects which aspect of Indian life?

A. Pure Western literary traditions

B. Scientific rationalism

C. Inner emotional, spiritual, and cultural experiences

D. Political propaganda

Answer: C

2. Which of the following is commonly used as imagery in Indian English poetry?

A. Industrial machines

B. Space technology

C. Rivers, seasons, rituals, and festivals

D. Abstract mathematical symbols

Answer: C

3. Indian English poets often use English to express:

A. Cultural rejection

B. Colonial loyalty

C. Indian philosophical and spiritual thought

D. Only urban realities

Answer: C

4. The concept of *impermanence* in Indian English poetry refers to:

A. Permanent success

B. Material prosperity

C. The transient nature of life and experiences

D. Political instability

Answer: C

5. Which poetic form is commonly adopted by Indian poets while retaining Indian sensibility?

A. Epic poetry only

B. Free verse and sonnets

C. Ballads exclusively

D. Dramatic monologues only

Answer: B

Short Answer Questions

1. What themes dominate Indian English poetry?
2. How is spirituality expressed in Indian English poetry?
3. What role does symbolism play in Indian English poems?
4. How do poets blend Indian sensibility with English form?
5. Why is introspection central to Indian English poetry?
6. How does poetry reflect Indian emotional life?

Long Answer Questions

1. Discuss the use of Indian imagery in English poetry.
2. Analyse the spiritual and philosophical depth of Indian English poetry.
3. Examine the fusion of Indian tradition and modern poetic forms.
4. Poetry expresses both personal and collective identity-discuss.
5. How does Indian English poetry reflect inner consciousness?
6. Evaluate Indian English poetry as a cultural expression.

5

Indian Drama in English – Stage as Social Conscience

5.1 Emergence of Indian Drama in English

Indian drama in English developed as writers sought new platforms to address social and political concerns. Theatre provided a public space where English could be used to communicate reformist ideas and cultural critique. This genre reflects the Indian mind's ability to adapt English for performative and socially engaged expression.

Indian drama in English emerged as a distinct literary and performative form during the late colonial and early postcolonial periods, when Indian writers began to view theatre as a powerful medium for public engagement. Unlike poetry or fiction, drama directly addresses an audience, making it especially suitable for expressing social concerns, political critique, and reformist ideas. English, already established as a language of administration and education, was gradually adapted by dramatists to reach urban, educated audiences while still reflecting Indian realities.

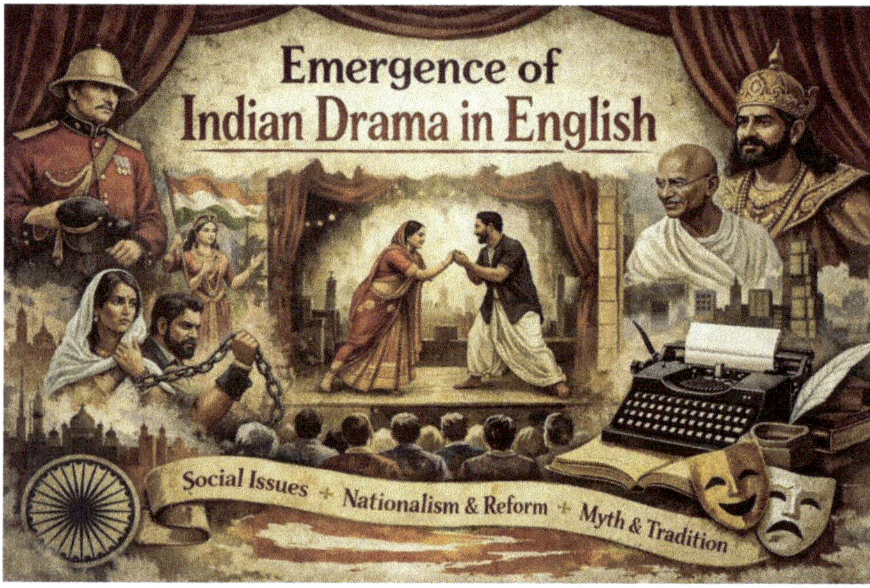

The growth of Indian drama in English was closely linked to social reform movements and nationalist consciousness. Playwrights used the stage to question social evils such as caste discrimination, gender inequality, blind tradition, and colonial dominance. Theatre halls became spaces for dialogue, debate, and awareness, where English functioned not merely as a borrowed language but as a tool reshaped to convey Indian emotions, conflicts, and values. Through dialogue, symbolism, and character portrayal, dramatists infused English with Indian rhythms, idioms, and cultural references.

Another significant aspect of this emergence is the performative nature of Indian drama in English. While the language was English, the themes, settings, and dramatic structures often drew from Indian history, mythology, and contemporary social life. This blending created a hybrid theatrical form that balanced Western dramatic techniques with Indian storytelling traditions. The result was drama that spoke to Indian audiences while also being accessible to global readers and viewers.

Overall, the emergence of Indian drama in English reflects the adaptability and creativity of the Indian mind. By transforming English into a medium of performance and social engagement, Indian dramatists demonstrated that the language could express collective concerns, cultural critique, and lived realities. Indian drama in English thus stands as a testament to cultural negotiation, where a global language is reshaped to serve local voices and societal transformation.

5.2 Theatre as a Medium for Social Critique

Indian playwrights use drama to highlight issues such as social injustice, gender inequality, and moral conflict. Through dialogue and character interaction, English drama exposes contradictions within society. The stage becomes a site where Indian consciousness questions tradition, authority, and social norms.

In Indian drama written in English, theatre functions as a powerful medium for social critique by bringing pressing social issues into a shared public space. Playwrights consciously use the stage to reflect realities such as social injustice, gender discrimination, economic inequality, and ethical dilemmas that shape everyday life. Unlike abstract literary forms, drama presents these concerns through living characters and visible conflicts, allowing audiences to witness social problems as lived experiences rather than distant ideas.

Dialogue plays a central role in exposing contradictions within society. Through conversations, arguments, and confrontations between characters, playwrights reveal tensions between tradition and modernity, authority and resistance, morality and hypocrisy. English, when used in dramatic dialogue, becomes a flexible tool that carries Indian thought patterns, emotional depth, and cultural nuance. The spoken word on stage often mirrors social interactions, making the critique more immediate and impactful.

Theatre also allows Indian consciousness to openly question long-established social norms and power structures. Customs related to caste, patriarchy, religion, and political control are examined critically through plot and characterization. By placing these issues in a performative setting, playwrights encourage audiences to reflect on their own beliefs and roles within society. The stage thus becomes a space of moral inquiry, where social values are tested rather than passively accepted.

Overall, theatre in Indian English drama serves not merely as entertainment but as a mirror and a challenge to society. It transforms performance into a form of social commentary, where collective anxieties, injustices, and aspirations are voiced. Through these medium, Indian playwrights use English to question authority, reinterpret tradition, and promote social awareness, reinforcing theatre's role as an agent of critical thought and cultural reflection.

5.3 Cultural Context and Indigenous Themes

Despite being written in English, Indian drama often draws from local myths, history, and folk traditions. Characters, settings, and conflicts reflect Indian social realities. This grounding in indigenous context ensures that English drama remains culturally authentic while addressing universal concerns.

Indian drama in English remains deeply rooted in indigenous culture despite its use of a foreign language. Playwrights consistently draw inspiration from local myths, historical events, folk traditions, and regional social practices to shape their dramatic worlds. This cultural grounding ensures that the plays reflect Indian life in its complexity, drawing upon shared memories, beliefs, and value systems that resonate strongly with Indian audiences. English, in this context, functions as a medium of expression rather than a determinant of cultural identity.

Characters in Indian English drama are often modelled on recognizable social types-traditional elders, reform-minded youth, marginalized voices, and conflicted individuals navigating social change. Their struggles reflect real Indian social conditions such as caste hierarchies, family obligations, gender roles, religious diversity, and rural–urban tensions. Settings frequently mirror familiar spaces like homes, temples, streets, villages, or urban neighbourhoods, reinforcing the sense of cultural authenticity. Through these elements, drama captures the lived experiences of Indian society rather than abstract or imported realities.

Indigenous storytelling traditions also influence dramatic structure and themes. Elements of mythology, folklore, and oral performance-such as symbolic characters, moral dilemmas, and cyclical narratives-are often woven into modern dramatic forms. This blending allows playwrights to address timeless human concerns like justice, identity, conflict, and reconciliation while anchoring them firmly in Indian cultural frameworks. As a result, the plays speak simultaneously to local sensibilities and broader human experiences.

By grounding English drama in cultural context and indigenous themes, Indian playwrights ensure that their work remains both authentic and relevant. The use of English does not dilute cultural identity; instead, it becomes a bridge that carries Indian realities to wider audiences. This balance between local roots and universal concerns gives Indian drama in English its distinctive voice-one that reflects the richness of Indian culture while engaging with global literary traditions.

Case Study: Cultural Context and Indigenous Themes in Indian Drama in English

Case Study: Girish Karnad's *Hayavadana*

Hayavadana by Girish Karnad is a classic case study that illustrates how Indian drama in English remains culturally authentic through indigenous themes. Although written in English, the play draws heavily from Indian mythology, particularly a story from the *Kathasaritsagara*, and integrates elements of folk theatre such as the *Yakshagana* tradition. This fusion of myth, folklore, and modern drama highlights how English can be adapted to express deeply Indian cultural narratives.

The play explores philosophical and social questions related to identity, completeness, and human desire through symbolic characters and mythic situations. The figure of Hayavadana-a man with a horse's head-comes from folk imagination and represents the human longing for wholeness. By using mythological symbolism, Karnad addresses universal concerns while grounding them in Indian cultural thought. The presence of a narrator-like *Bhagavata* further reinforces indigenous performance traditions within a modern theatrical framework.

Cultural authenticity is also evident in the social values and moral dilemmas portrayed in the play. Themes such as the conflict between intellect and physical strength, marital expectations, and the limits of human perfection reflect Indian philosophical ideas rather than Western dramatic conventions alone. The language may be English, but the emotional rhythms, narrative logic, and symbolic meanings are rooted in Indian worldview and storytelling practices.

This case study demonstrates that Indian drama in English does not abandon its cultural roots. Instead, plays like *Hayavadana* show how indigenous myths, folk traditions, and social realities can coexist with a global language. The result is theatre that is culturally grounded, intellectually rich, and universally relevant-affirming that English drama in India can remain authentically Indian while engaging with broader human concerns.

5.4 Drama as Collective Experience and Awareness

Unlike solitary reading, theatre engages audiences directly, making social reflection a shared experience. Indian English drama encourages

collective thinking and dialogue. It transforms English into a language of public conscience, promoting awareness, empathy, and critical engagement.

Drama differs fundamentally from other literary forms because it is experienced collectively rather than privately. In Indian English drama, this collective dimension plays a crucial role in shaping social awareness. When a play is performed, audiences gather in a shared space and witness the unfolding of social conflicts, moral dilemmas, and human emotions together. This immediacy transforms theatre into a powerful platform for communal reflection, where ideas are not only understood intellectually but also felt emotionally.

Indian English drama uses this shared experience to stimulate dialogue and critical thinking. As audiences observe characters struggling with injustice, identity, tradition, or authority, they are encouraged to reflect on similar issues within their own social contexts. The reactions of laughter, silence, discomfort, or empathy are collectively experienced, reinforcing the sense that social problems are not individual concerns but shared responsibilities. Theatre thus becomes a space where society examines itself openly.

Drama as a Site of Resistance and Social Intervention

English, in this performative context, is reshaped into a language of public conscience. Rather than remaining an elite or academic medium, it becomes accessible, spoken, and socially engaged. Through dialogue, conflict, and resolution on stage, English carries the emotional weight of Indian experiences and social realities. This transformation allows English to function as a bridge between personal awareness and public discourse, fostering understanding across diverse audiences.

Ultimately, drama in Indian English literature promotes awareness by cultivating empathy and moral engagement. By presenting lived experiences before a collective audience, theatre encourages viewers to question assumptions, challenge social norms, and consider alternative perspectives. In doing so, Indian English drama elevates theatre beyond entertainment, turning it into a shared act of social consciousness and an instrument for collective ethical reflection.

5.5 Drama as a Site of Resistance and Social Intervention

Indian English drama goes beyond representation to actively intervene in social realities. .

It does not merely mirror society but questions, disrupts, and resists dominant structures of power. Through staging conflict, dissent, and alternative viewpoints, drama becomes a site where marginalized voices find articulation and where entrenched norms are challenged in public view. This capacity for resistance gives Indian English drama a distinctly transformative role within literature and society

Theatre has historically been linked with protest and reform, and Indian English drama continues this tradition by addressing issues such as colonial legacies, gender inequality, caste hierarchies, political corruption, and cultural alienation. Playwrights use dramatic conflict to expose contradictions within social systems—between law and justice, tradition and individual freedom, authority and conscience. By dramatizing these tensions, the stage becomes a space where unquestioned assumptions are unsettled, and audiences are invited to reconsider accepted truths.

What distinguishes drama as a form of social intervention is its immediacy. Unlike abstract critique, theatrical resistance unfolds through living characters, spoken words, and visible consequences. Audiences witness acts of defiance, moral courage, and ethical struggle in real time, which can provoke discomfort as well as reflection. This lived quality of performance enables drama to reach beyond intellectual agreement and create emotional and ethical engagement with social issues.

Language plays a crucial role in this process of resistance. In Indian English drama, English is adapted to convey dissent rooted in local realities. The language carries irony, satire, anger, and hope, allowing playwrights to critique power while still engaging diverse audiences. English thus becomes a tool not of domination but of questioning—capable of challenging authority and amplifying suppressed perspectives.

By functioning as a site of resistance, Indian English drama asserts the social responsibility of literature. It reminds audiences that art can intervene in public life, encourage critical awareness, and inspire change. Drama, in this sense, is not only a cultural expression but also a form of social action, positioning the stage as a space where conscience, critique, and collective responsibility intersect.

Multiple Choice Questions (MCQs)

1. The emergence of Indian drama in English was primarily influenced by:

a) Romantic poetry traditions

b) Social reform movements and public engagement

c) Courtly entertainment in ancient India

d) Purely Western theatrical models

Answer: b) Social reform movements and public engagement

2. Why is theatre considered an effective medium for social critique in Indian English drama?

a) It focuses mainly on entertainment

b) It allows private reflection without audience involvement

c) It presents social issues through live interaction and dialogue

d) It avoids controversial subjects

Answer: c) It presents social issues through live interaction and dialogue

3. Indian English playwrights often use dialogue to:

a) Decorate language with poetic imagery only

b) Expose social contradictions and moral conflicts

c) Maintain strict classical rules

d) Avoid addressing social realities

Answer: b) Expose social contradictions and moral conflicts

4. Which of the following themes is commonly addressed in Indian drama in English?

a) Fantasy without social relevance

b) Social injustice and gender inequality

c) Mythology without reinterpretation

d) Pure escapism

Answer: b) Social injustice and gender inequality

5. Despite being written in English, Indian drama remains culturally authentic because it:

a) Imitates Western lifestyles

b) Avoids indigenous references

c) Draws from local myths, history, and social realities

d) Focuses only on elite urban characters

Answer: c) Draws from local myths, history, and social realities

Short Answer Questions

1. Why did Indian drama in English emerge?
2. What social issues are addressed in Indian English drama?
3. Why is theatre an effective medium for critique?
4. How does dialogue shape dramatic expression?
5. What role does culture play in Indian English drama?

Long Answer Questions

1. Discuss the development of Indian drama in English.
2. Analyse theatre as a platform for social criticism.
3. Examine the role of drama in questioning social norms.
4. How does Indian English drama reflect cultural realities?
5. Drama as a collective social experience-discuss.

6

Postcolonial Rewriting and Resistance

6.1 Reclaiming Voice After Colonialism

Postcolonial Indian writers use English to reclaim narrative authority. Rather than accepting colonial perspectives, they reinterpret history and experience from indigenous viewpoints. Writing becomes an act of intellectual independence, demonstrating how English can be repurposed to express self-defined identity.

Aspect	Colonial Representation	Postcolonial Reinterpretation
Control over Narrative	History and culture described from an external, colonial viewpoint	Indian writers assert authority over their own stories and experiences
Use of English	English imposed as a language of administration and power	English reshaped as a medium of self-expression and resistance
Portrayal of Identity	Indians often depicted as passive, inferior, or exotic	Identity presented as complex, self-defined, and culturally grounded
Historical Perspective	Emphasis on imperial achievements and dominance	Focus on indigenous memory, resistance, and lived realities
Cultural Representation	Local traditions marginalized or misunderstood	Indigenous values, customs, and voices brought to the centre

After the end of British rule, Indian writers faced the complex task of expressing their realities in a language once associated with domination. Instead of rejecting English, many postcolonial Indian writers deliberately chose to **reclaim and reshape it**. English became a tool for asserting agency rather than submission. By writing in English on their own terms, these writers challenged colonial narratives that had long portrayed India through external, often distorted lenses.

Postcolonial Indian writing reinterprets history from **indigenous perspectives**. Colonial accounts frequently emphasized imperial superiority while marginalizing local voices, traditions, and experiences. Indian writers counter this imbalance by retelling historical events, social practices, and cultural memories from within the community. Through novels, essays, and poetry, they recover silenced stories-of resistance, everyday life, and inner conflict-thereby restoring narrative ownership to those who were previously spoken for rather than heard.

Using English also allows Indian writers to **address both national and global audiences**. While the language is global, the vision it carries is rooted in local realities-village life, caste dynamics, spiritual traditions, and post-independence struggles. Writers adapt English to Indian rhythms, expressions, and thought patterns, transforming it into a medium capable of carrying Indian sensibilities. This adaptation demonstrates that English no longer belongs exclusively to its colonial origins but can function as an Indian language of expression.

Ultimately, reclaiming voice through English represents an act of **intellectual and cultural independence**. Postcolonial Indian writers assert the right to define themselves, their past, and their future without external validation.

Writing becomes a form of resistance as well as self-definition, proving that a once-imposed language can be reworked into a powerful instrument of identity, dignity, and creative freedom.

6.2 Challenging Colonial Narratives

This section examines how Indian writers question colonial stereotypes and assumptions embedded in earlier literature. Through irony, reinterpretation, and alternative storytelling, English is used to expose historical distortions. The Indian mind reshapes language to challenge inherited power structures.

Colonial literature often presented India through fixed stereotypes-portraying it as backward, passive, mystical, or incapable of self-governance. These representations were not neutral; they supported imperial authority by shaping how India was understood by both colonizers and the colonized. Indian writers writing in English actively challenge these inherited assumptions by questioning the ideological foundations of colonial narratives and exposing their biases.

One important strategy used by Indian writers is **reinterpretation**. Historical events, social customs, and cultural practices that were earlier described from a colonial viewpoint are retold from within Indian experience. By shifting the perspective, writers reveal how colonial texts often distorted reality to justify domination. What appeared as "civilizing missions" in colonial accounts are re-examined as systems of exploitation, control, and cultural suppression.

Irony and satire also play a crucial role in dismantling colonial authority. Indian writers frequently use subtle humour, reversal, and irony to highlight the contradictions and arrogance within colonial thinking. By mimicking or parodying colonial language and attitudes, they expose how claims of moral or intellectual superiority were often hollow. This technique allows writers to undermine power without direct confrontation, making resistance both creative and intellectually sharp.

Alternative storytelling methods further help in challenging dominant narratives. Instead of linear, official histories favoured by colonial discourse, Indian writers emphasize memory, oral traditions, personal experiences, and marginalized voices. These narrative choices disrupt the idea that colonial history is the only valid version of the past. English, once a language of control, is reshaped to carry dissent, critique, and reinterpretation.

Through these approaches, the **Indian mind transforms English into a counter-discursive tool**. Language becomes a site of struggle where inherited power structures are questioned and reworked. Challenging colonial narratives is not merely about correcting history; it is about reclaiming the right to think, interpret, and represent reality independently. In this way, Indian writers turn English literature into a space of resistance, critical awareness, and cultural self-assertion.

Dimension	Colonial Narratives	Indian Writers' Response
View of India	Presented as backward, passive, or exotic	Portrayed as complex, dynamic, and historically conscious
Cultural Stereotypes	Indians shown as irrational or inferior	Stereotypes questioned and dismantled through critical representation
Historical Interpretation	Colonial rule justified as a civilizing mission	History reinterpreted as a period of control, exploitation, and resistance
Narrative Techniques	Linear, authoritative, official histories	Use of irony, memory, oral tradition, and alternative viewpoints
Language Function	English used to reinforce power and dominance	English reshaped as a medium of critique and resistance
Power Structures	Colonial authority presented as natural and unquestionable	Inherited power structures exposed and challenged

Authorial Position	Colonizer speaks for the colonized	Indian writers speak for themselves and marginalized voices

6.3 Hybridity and Cultural Assertion

Postcolonial writing reflects cultural hybridity, where multiple influences coexist. Indian writers do not reject English outright but transform it through cultural assertion. This hybrid expression reflects confidence rather than dependency, showing English as a tool of negotiation rather than dominance.

ostcolonial Indian writing is shaped by **cultural hybridity** , a condition in which indigenous traditions and global influences exist together rather than in opposition. English, once introduced through colonial rule, becomes part of this blended cultural space. Indian writers do not treat the language as a symbol of submission; instead, they engage with it creatively, allowing local values, memories, and social realities to reshape its form and meaning.

Hybridity in Indian English literature is not about cultural loss but about **cultural assertion** . Writers infuse English with Indian idioms, metaphors, rhythms of speech, and references drawn from everyday life. Festivals, myths, family structures, and social hierarchies appear naturally within English narratives, demonstrating that Indian culture remains central even when expressed in a global language. This process ensures that English carries Indian thought patterns rather than replacing them.

Such hybrid expression reflects **confidence rather than dependence** . Indian writers use English consciously, aware of its history but not constrained by it. By blending languages, traditions, and narrative styles, they assert control over expression and identity. The coexistence of multiple influences mirrors the lived reality of postcolonial India, where tradition and modernity interact continuously.

Importantly, hybridity turns English into a tool of negotiation rather than dominance. It allows writers to communicate across cultural boundaries while maintaining authenticity. Through hybrid writing, Indian authors demonstrate that identity is not fixed or pure but dynamic and evolving. English literature thus becomes a space where cultural self-assurance is affirmed, power relations are rebalanced, and postcolonial voices articulate their presence with clarity and authority.

6.4 Resistance Through Literary Expression

Literature becomes a form of resistance when it questions injustice and affirms cultural dignity. Indian English writing address's themes of marginalization, identity, and autonomy. By reshaping English to express resistance, writers demonstrate the resilience and adaptability of Indian consciousness.

In postcolonial Indian writing, literature functions as a powerful form of resistance. Rather than being limited to artistic expression alone, writing becomes a means of questioning injustice, exposing inequality, and asserting cultural dignity. Indian writers use English to confront social, political, and historical realities that have shaped experiences of oppression, silence, and exclusion. Through this process, literature transforms into a voice of protest and self-affirmation.

Indian English writing frequently engages with themes of marginalization and identity. Issues such as caste discrimination, gender inequality, poverty, displacement, and cultural alienation are brought to the foreground. By giving narrative space to voices that were historically ignored or misrepresented, writers challenge dominant power structures. These literary representations resist not only colonial legacies but also internal systems of domination that continue to shape society.

Resistance is also expressed through the **creative reshaping of English** . Writers adapt the language to reflect Indian realities, emotions, and modes of thought. Local expressions, cultural symbols, and non-Western narrative styles disrupt standardized English forms, signalling refusal to conform to inherited norms. This linguistic transformation itself becomes an act of resistance, proving that English can no longer dictate meaning or authority.

Ultimately, resistance through literary expression highlights the **resilience and adaptability of Indian consciousness** . Indian writers demonstrate that despite historical domination, cultural identity remains dynamic and self-renewing. Literature becomes a space where dignity is reclaimed, autonomy is asserted, and resistance is articulated with intellectual depth and moral strength. Through English, Indian writing turns a former instrument of control into a vehicle for endurance, critique, and cultural self-respect.

Multiple Choice Questions (MCQs)

1. What is the primary aim of postcolonial rewriting in Indian English literature?

A. To imitate Western literary styles

B. To preserve colonial viewpoints

C. To reclaim narrative authority from colonial discourse

D. To reject English completely

Answer: C

2. How do postcolonial Indian writers primarily use the English language?

A. As a symbol of submission

B. As a neutral medium without history

C. As a tool for resistance and self-expression

D. As a replacement for Indian languages

Answer: C

3. Colonial narratives often portrayed India as:

A. Progressive and self-reliant

B. Backward and dependent

C. Economically dominant

D. Politically autonomous

Answer: B

4. Which literary technique is commonly used to challenge colonial authority?

A. Literal translation

B. Excessive formalism

C. Irony and reinterpretation

D. Silence and avoidance

Answer: C

5. What does cultural hybridity signify in postcolonial Indian writing?

A. Cultural confusion

B. Loss of identity

C. Coexistence of indigenous and global influences

D. Total Westernization

Answer: C

Short Answer Questions

1. What is postcolonial literature?
2. How do writers reclaim voice after colonialism?
3. What is meant by resistance in literature?
4. Define hybridity in postcolonial writing.
5. How are colonial narratives challenged?
6. Why is English used in postcolonial resistance?

Long Answer Questions

1. Discuss postcolonial resistance in Indian English literature.
2. Analyse how English becomes a language of resistance.
3. Examine hybridity as a key feature of postcolonial writing.
4. How do Indian writers rewrite colonial history?
5. Literature functions as cultural resistance-discuss.
6. Evaluate the transformation of English in postcolonial India.

7

Feminist Voices and Gendered Consciousness

7.1 Emergence of Women's Voices in Indian English Literature

Indian women writers using English brought previously silenced experiences into literary discourse.

Writing in English enabled them to articulate inner lives, domestic realities, and social constraints faced by women. Their work marks a shift from marginal representation to self-assertion, where women speak *for themselves* rather than being spoken *about*.

The emergence of women's voices in Indian English literature represents a decisive transformation in both theme and perspective. For a long time, women in Indian literary texts were depicted largely through male viewpoints, often confined to idealized or stereotypical roles. When women themselves began writing in English, the language became a powerful medium of self-expression rather than mere representation. English provided access to a wider readership and offered a relatively neutral space to question traditions, examine gender roles, and articulate experiences that were often silenced within patriarchal social structures.

Indian women writers used literature to explore the *inner lives* of women-areas such as emotional conflict, loneliness, marital dissatisfaction, identity crises, and the tension between personal desire and social expectation. Domestic spaces, which had earlier been treated as insignificant or purely private, were reimagined as sites of psychological struggle and quiet resistance. Through introspection and subtle narration, these writers revealed how everyday life itself could be a source of oppression as well as resilience.

Indian English Literature

This shift also marked a move from marginality to self-assertion. Women were no longer passive subjects in stories shaped by others; they became active narrators of their own realities. Their writing challenged the notion that women's experiences were secondary or unworthy of serious literary attention. Instead, personal emotions, mental states, and domestic negotiations were presented as complex and meaningful aspects of human existence.

7.2 Representation of Domestic Space and Female Experience

Indian feminist writing in English often redefines the domestic sphere as a site of conflict, resistance, and identity formation. Household relationships, marriage, motherhood, and silence are explored as social structures that shape women's consciousness. English becomes a language through which everyday female experiences gain literary and intellectual legitimacy.

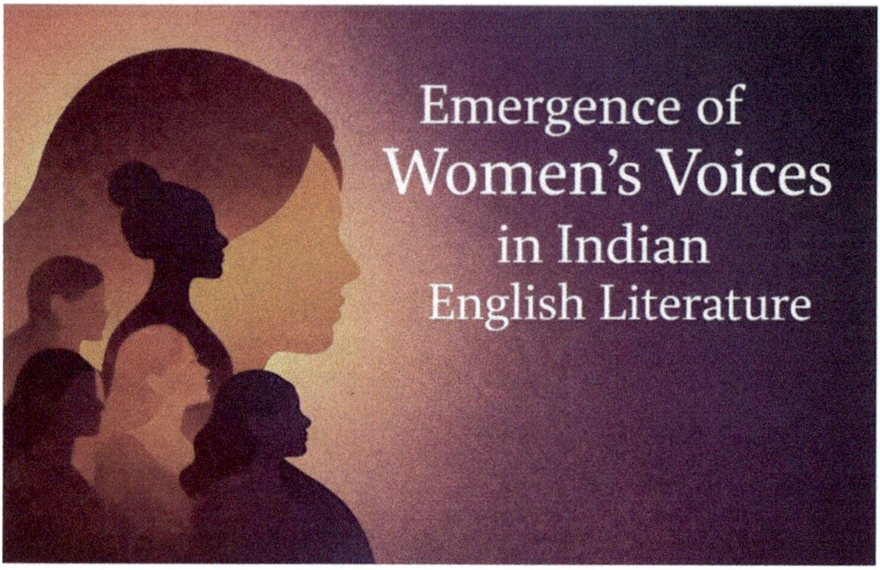

Indian feminist writing in English brings renewed attention to the domestic sphere, transforming it from a background setting into a central site of meaning. Traditionally viewed as private, apolitical, or insignificant, the home is reimagined as a space where power relations are enacted daily. Household routines, family hierarchies, and gendered expectations become crucial in shaping women's identities, emotions, and worldviews. By focusing on domestic life, women writers reveal that personal spaces are deeply connected to broader social and cultural structures.

Marriage, motherhood, and family roles are frequently portrayed not merely as natural stages of life but as social institutions that regulate women's choices and behaviour. Silence-often expected from women in the name of harmony or respect-is shown as a powerful symbol of suppression, endurance, and sometimes quiet resistance. Through reflective narration and psychological insight, writers expose how emotional labour, sacrifice, and conformity are normalized within the home, even as they limit personal growth and freedom.

Writing in English allows these everyday female experiences to gain literary and intellectual legitimacy. The language becomes a tool to analyse, question, and reinterpret domestic realities that were once dismissed as trivial. By articulating inner conflicts and unspoken frustrations, Indian women writers elevate domestic experiences to subjects worthy of serious reflection, thereby challenging the boundary between the private and the public.

Case Illustration: Many narratives depict female protagonists negotiating expectations within joint family systems. These characters often struggle to balance personal aspirations with traditional duties, revealing how cultural norms and family authority can restrict autonomy. Such portrayals highlight the tension between belonging and individuality, showing that the domestic space is not merely a place of shelter but also a complex arena of constraint, negotiation, and self-definition.

7.3 Challenging Patriarchy Through Narrative

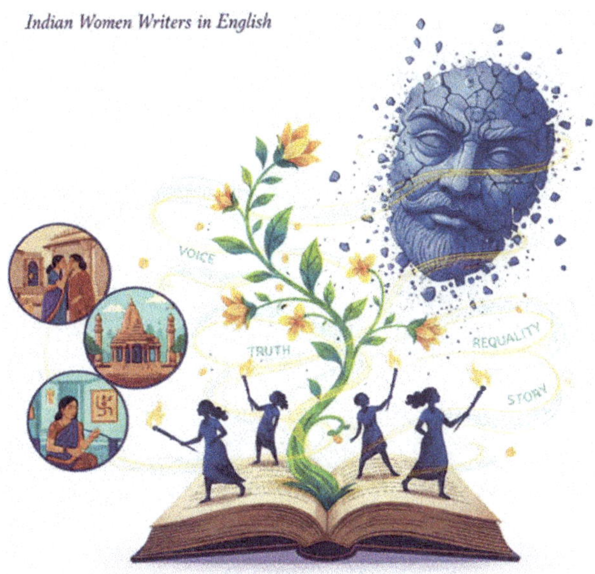

Women writers employ English to question patriarchal authority embedded in culture, religion, and social customs. Through narrative voice, symbolism, and interior monologue, they expose gender inequality and emotional suppression. Literature thus becomes a space for critique rather than compliance.

Indian women writers in English actively use narrative as a form of resistance against patriarchal authority embedded in culture, religion, and everyday social practices. Rather than confronting power only through overt rebellion, they challenge it through *storytelling itself*. By choosing who speaks, what is remembered, and how emotions are expressed, these writers disrupt traditional hierarchies that privilege male authority and silence female experience. English becomes a strategic medium through which critique can reach both national and global audiences, expanding the impact of feminist discourse.

Narrative techniques such as **interior monologue**, **symbolism**, and **fragmented storytelling** allow writers to expose the invisible forms of oppression that shape women's lives. Emotional suppression, unfulfilled desire, fear, and internalized obedience are revealed as consequences of patriarchal conditioning rather than personal weakness. By foregrounding women's inner voices, these narratives question the moral and cultural legitimacy of systems that demand silence, sacrifice, and submission from women in the name of tradition or honour.

Literature, in this context, moves beyond mere representation to become a space of critique. Stories challenge dominant myths about family, gender roles, and social order, revealing how power operates subtly through customs and beliefs. The act of narrating women's pain, anger, and resistance itself becomes political, asserting that personal experiences are inseparable from social and structural inequalities.

7.4 Feminist Writing as Social Transformation

Feminist Indian English literature does not merely reflect women's suffering; it also imagines transformation. By asserting agency, questioning norms, and redefining identity, these texts influence social thought. English functions as a medium through which gendered consciousness enters global feminist discourse while remaining rooted in Indian realities.

Feminist writing in Indian English literature moves beyond documenting women's suffering to actively imagining possibilities of change. These texts do not position women only as victims of social structures; instead, they foreground women as thinking, questioning, and decision-making individuals. By asserting agency and self-awareness, feminist writers challenge inherited norms related to marriage, family, sexuality, and social obedience, encouraging readers to reconsider what is often accepted as "natural" or inevitable in women's lives.

A significant contribution of this literature lies in its redefinition of female identity. Women characters are portrayed as evolving subjects who negotiate tradition and modernity rather than being confined to fixed roles. Acts such as self-expression, refusal, emotional honesty, and even silence is depicted as forms of resistance. Through these representations, literature becomes a site where alternative social arrangements and more equitable relationships are imagined, suggesting that personal transformation can lead to broader social change.

Writing in English allows Indian feminist voices to participate in global feminist conversations while retaining a strong connection to local realities. The language becomes a bridge rather than a barrier-carrying experiences shaped by caste, class, religion, and family structures into an international literary space. In doing so, Indian feminist writing resists homogenized Western feminist models and asserts a distinct, context-sensitive feminist consciousness.

As a result, feminist Indian English literature influences social thought by reshaping attitudes toward gender, power, and individuality. It sensitizes readers to hidden inequalities, legitimizes women's perspectives, and encourages critical reflection on social practices. Through imagination, critique, and narrative innovation, feminist writing contributes to social transformation by envisioning a society in which women's voices are central, acknowledged, and transformative.

Multiple Choice Questions (MCQs)

1. What is a key contribution of feminist voices in Indian English literature?

A. Reinforcing traditional gender roles

B. Highlighting male dominance as natural

C. Bringing women lived experiences into literary discourse

D. Avoiding social issues

Answer: C

2. Indian feminist writing often redefines the domestic space as a site of:

A. Comfort and harmony only

B. Political indifference

C. Conflict, resistance, and identity formation

D. Escape from society

Answer: C

3. Why is English an important medium for Indian feminist writers?

A. It replaces Indian languages

B. It limits local expression

C. It provides global reach and critical distance

D. It discourages cultural specificity

Answer: C

4. Which narrative technique is commonly used by women writers to expose inner conflict?

A. Epic narration

B. Interior monologue

C. Mythological allegory only

D. Dramatic dialogue alone

Answer: B

5. The shift in women's writing from marginality to self-assertion means that women:

A. Are portrayed mainly as passive figures

B. Speak for themselves rather than being spoken about

C. Avoid social criticism

D. Focus only on external action

Answer: B

Short Answer Questions

1. What is feminist literary criticism?

2. How do women writers represent domestic space?

3. Why is English important for feminist expression in India?

4. What themes dominate feminist Indian English writing?

5. How is patriarchy questioned in literature?

6. What is meant by gendered consciousness?

Long Answer Questions

1. Discuss the emergence of feminist voices in Indian English literature.

2. Analyse women's inner lives as portrayed in Indian English writing.

3. Examine how feminist writing challenges patriarchy.

4. Literature as a tool of women's empowerment-discuss.

5. Evaluate feminist writing as a force for social change.

6. How does feminist literature reshape Indian consciousness?

8

Diaspora, Globalization, and Transnational Indian English

8.1 Migration and the Experience of Displacement

Diasporic Indian writers in English explore the emotional impact of migration, including loss, nostalgia, and cultural dislocation. English serves as a shared linguistic space for expressing the tension between homeland and host land. The migrant experience reshapes Indian consciousness through distance and reflection.

Migration occupies a central place in diasporic Indian writing in English, as it captures the deep emotional and psychological consequences of leaving one's homeland and adapting to a new cultural environment. For Indian writers living outside India, migration is not merely a physical movement across borders, but an inner journey marked by feelings of loss, nostalgia, alienation, and uncertainty. The homeland often exists in memory-as a place of emotional attachment, traditions, and belonging-while the host land represents opportunity alongside cultural unfamiliarity and social distance. This duality creates a sense of displacement, where migrants feel suspended between two worlds without complete belonging to either.

English plays a crucial role in articulating this experience of displacement. As a shared global language, it becomes a medium through which writers express the tension between past and present, roots and routes. Although English may not be the writer's mother tongue, it provides the expressive space to reflect on fragmented identities shaped by migration. Through English, diasporic writers translate cultural memories, native customs, and emotional conflicts into a language that can communicate across borders, thereby transforming personal experiences into universal narratives.

Diasporic stories frequently portray migrants struggling with cultural adjustment in everyday life-workplaces, social interactions, family relationships, and generational conflicts. These narratives reveal how identity becomes fluid rather than fixed. Migrants constantly negotiate who they are, adapting to new cultural norms while attempting to preserve elements of their original identity. This process often leads to hybrid identities, where individuals belong simultaneously to multiple cultures yet feel fully settled in none.

Importantly, migration reshapes Indian consciousness through distance and reflection. Being away from the homeland allows writers to view Indian culture with both affection and critical insight. Displacement sharpens awareness of tradition, language, and belonging, encouraging introspection about what it truly means to be "Indian" in a global context. Thus, diasporic Indian writing transforms migration from a story of loss alone into a space of self-discovery, cultural negotiation, and evolving identity, reflecting the dynamic nature of Indian consciousness in the modern world.

8.2 Hyphenated Identity and Cultural Memory

Diasporic literature often reflects hyphenated identities-Indian-American, Indian-British-where individuals belong to multiple cultural worlds. Writers use English to preserve cultural memory while engaging with global realities. Food, rituals, language fragments, and family history become anchors of identity.

Diasporic Indian literature in English frequently explores the idea of *hyphenated identity*, expressed through terms such as Indian-American or Indian-British. These identities represent lives shaped by more than one cultural inheritance, where individuals simultaneously belong to their ancestral culture and their adopted national context. Rather than suggesting division, the hyphen symbolizes coexistence-an ongoing negotiation between multiple cultural worlds. Diasporic writers portray identity as layered and dynamic, formed through everyday choices, memories, and social interactions across borders.

English becomes a vital literary tool in expressing this complex identity. While it is often the dominant language of the host country, writers reshape English to carry cultural memory from the homeland. Through English narratives, they preserve traditions, values, and emotional ties associated with India while also engaging with modern, global realities. The language thus functions as a bridge-connecting inherited cultural pasts with contemporary lived experiences.

Cultural memory in diasporic writing is frequently anchored in intimate, everyday elements. Food becomes a powerful symbol of belonging, carrying the tastes and smells of home across generations. Rituals such as festivals, weddings, and religious practices reinforce continuity with ancestral traditions. Fragments of Indian languages embedded within English prose-words, phrases, or expressions-serve as emotional markers of origin. Family histories, stories of migration, and generational memories further strengthen identity by linking individuals to a collective past, even when physical distance separates them from the homeland.

A notable case study is **Jhumpa Lahiri**, whose works vividly portray second-generation immigrants negotiating hyphenated identities. Her characters often struggle to balance parental expectations rooted in Indian tradition with the cultural norms of their Western surroundings. They experience feelings of cultural fragmentation-belonging fully to neither world-yet they also demonstrate resilience by crafting identities that draw strength from both. Lahiri's narratives highlight how cultural memory sustains individuals, allowing them to reinterpret tradition rather than abandon it.

Overall, diasporic literature presents hyphenated identity not as a crisis but as a creative space. By preserving cultural memory through language, rituals, and family narratives, writers show that identity can be multiple, adaptive, and enduring-capable of honouring the past while embracing the present.

8.3 Global English and Indian Sensibility

In diasporic writing, English becomes a global language shaped by Indian sensibility. Writers infuse English with Indian cultural references, emotional patterns, and social values. This transformation shows that globalization does not erase cultural identity but reshapes its expression.

In diasporic Indian writing, English emerges not as a neutral or uniform global language but as one deeply shaped by Indian sensibility. As Indian writers live and write across continents, they adapt English to express culturally specific emotions, values, and worldviews rooted in Indian experience. This process transforms English from a colonial or foreign medium into a flexible linguistic space capable of carrying Indian thought, memory, and social meaning.

Diasporic writers infuse English with Indian cultural references drawn from everyday life-family structures, religious practices, festivals, food habits, and social customs. These references are often presented without translation or explanation, asserting cultural confidence and signalling that Indian experience does not need validation from Western norms. Alongside these references, emotional patterns characteristic of Indian sensibility-such as strong family attachment, respect for elders, collective responsibility, and moral reflection-shape narrative tone and character relationships. Through such infusions, English becomes emotionally resonant with Indian cultural rhythms.

Social values also play a key role in reshaping global English. Diasporic narratives frequently emphasize community bonds, intergenerational duty, and ethical dilemmas rooted in cultural tradition. Even when characters live in highly individualistic societies, their responses to conflict often reflect Indian value systems. This blending of linguistic form and cultural content demonstrates that identity persists even in globalized contexts, adapting rather than disappearing.

Importantly, this transformation of English challenges the assumption that globalization leads to cultural homogenization. Instead, diasporic writing reveals globalization as a dialogic process, where languages absorb diverse cultural influences. English, in this context, becomes plural and multicultural-capable of reflecting multiple histories and sensibilities simultaneously. Indian writers reshape English to suit their expressive needs, proving that global communication does not require cultural erasure.

Thus, global English in diasporic literature becomes a site of creative negotiation. By embedding Indian sensibility within a global language, writers assert cultural continuity while engaging with the wider world. The result is a hybrid literary expression that honours Indian identity even as it participates fully in global discourse, reinforcing the idea that cultural identity evolves through interaction rather than loss.

Aspect	Description
Meaning of Global English	English used worldwide as a common language, adapted by different cultures rather than remaining uniform or Western-centric
Indian Sensibility	Emotional patterns, cultural values, traditions, and social attitudes rooted in Indian life and worldview
Language Transformation	Indian writers reshape English by embedding Indian idioms, cultural references, and emotional expressions
Cultural References	Use of Indian food, rituals, festivals, family systems, and social customs within English narratives
Emotional Patterns	Emphasis on family bonds, collective identity, respect for elders, nostalgia, and moral reflection
Role of Globalization	Globalization reshapes cultural expression instead of erasing identity, allowing multiple voices within English
Literary Significance	English becomes a plural, multicultural language reflecting Indian consciousness in a global context

Outcome	A hybrid form of expression where Indian identity survives, adapts, and asserts itself through global English

8.4 Diasporic Literature as Cultural Bridge

Diasporic Indian English literature functions as a bridge between cultures, fostering cross-cultural understanding. It introduces Indian social realities to global audiences while re-examining Indian identity from an external perspective. The result is a multilayered literary consciousness shaped by movement and memory.

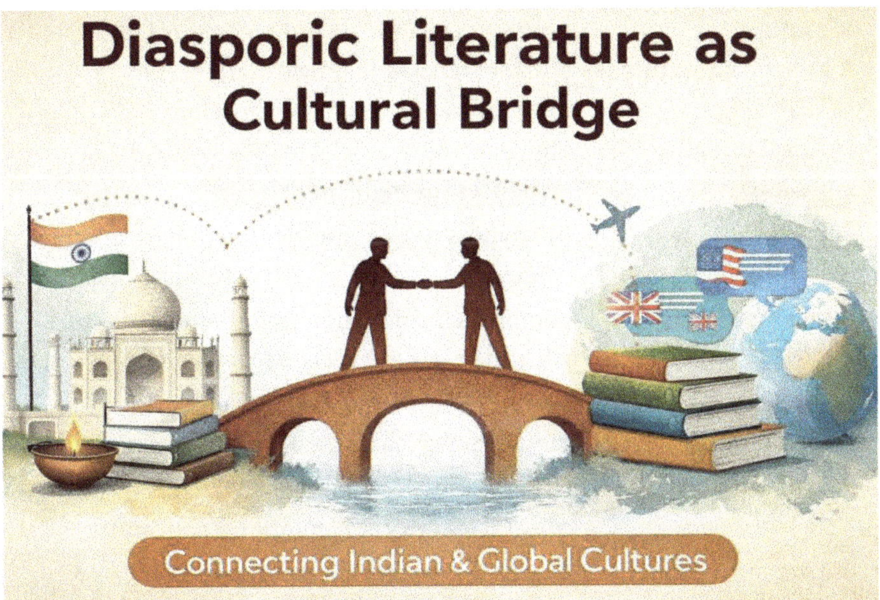

Diasporic Indian English literature plays a vital role as a cultural bridge, connecting Indian social realities with global audiences. Written from locations outside the homeland, this body of literature enables cultural exchange by translating Indian experiences, values, and traditions into a language understood worldwide. Through novels, short stories, essays, and memoirs, diasporic writers make Indian life accessible to readers unfamiliar with its social structures, emotional frameworks, and cultural practices.

One of the key functions of diasporic literature is its ability to present Indian society from both an insider's and an outsider's perspective. Writers draw upon lived memories of India-family life, customs, belief systems, and social hierarchies-while simultaneously interpreting them through the lens of distance and exposure to other cultures. This dual perspective allows for re-examination and critical reflection. Practices once taken for granted may be questioned, reinterpreted, or compared with those of the host culture, leading to deeper insights into identity and belonging.

Aspect	Explanation
Meaning of Diasporic Literature	Literature written by Indian writers living outside India, reflecting experiences of migration and cultural negotiation
Cultural Bridge Function	Connects Indian social realities with global audiences through English
Representation of Indian Society	Introduces Indian traditions, family structures, values, and social issues to non-Indian readers
Dual Perspective	Combines insider knowledge of Indian culture with an external, reflective viewpoint
Cross-Cultural Understanding	Promotes empathy by highlighting shared human experiences across cultures
Role of Memory	Uses recollections of homeland to preserve cultural identity and emotional continuity
Impact of Movement	Migration shape's identity, creating layered narratives of belonging and displacement
Literary Outcome	Produces a multilayered literary consciousness formed by movement, memory, and cultural dialogue

Diasporic texts often highlight cultural encounters and misunderstandings, showing how characters negotiate differences in language, behaviour, and values. These narratives encourage empathy by revealing shared human emotions such as longing, love, fear, and hope across cultural boundaries. As a result, readers from diverse backgrounds gain a more nuanced understanding of Indian culture, moving beyond stereotypes toward complex, humanized representations.

The movement inherent in diasporic life-across nations, languages, and traditions-creates a multilayered literary consciousness. Memory of the homeland interacts with present realities of migration, producing narratives rich in reflection and emotional depth. Indian identity in these works is not static; it evolves through displacement, adaptation, and cultural dialogue.

Ultimately, diasporic Indian English literature does more than tell migrant stories. It builds cultural connections, fosters mutual understanding, and expands the scope of Indian literature beyond geographical boundaries. By bridging cultures through movement and memory, it contributes to a global literary space where identities are shared, questioned, and continually reimagined.

Multiple Choice Questions (MCQs)

1. Diasporic Indian English literature primarily deals with

a) Colonial administration

b) Rural folklore only

c) Migration, identity, and cultural displacement

d) Mythological retellings

Answer: c) Migration, identity, and cultural displacement

2. The term "hyphenated identity" refers to

a) Linguistic errors in English

b) Divided national loyalty

c) Belonging to more than one cultural identity

d) Loss of cultural roots

Answer: c) Belonging to more than one cultural identity

3. English in diasporic Indian writing functions mainly as

a) A colonial imposition

b) A neutral global language

c) A cultural bridge and expressive medium

d) A replacement for Indian languages

Answer: c) A cultural bridge and expressive medium

4. Which of the following themes is commonly found in diasporic Indian literature?

a) Courtly romance

b) Nostalgia and memory of homeland

c) Medieval heroism

d) Scientific realism

Answer: b) Nostalgia and memory of homeland

5. Diasporic writers often infuse English with Indian sensibility by using

a) Purely Western idioms

b) Classical Latin expressions

c) Indian cultural references and emotional patterns

d) Technical vocabulary

Answer: c) Indian cultural references and emotional patterns

Short Answer Questions

1. What is diaspora literature?
2. How does migration affect identity?
3. What is a hyphenated identity?
4. Why is memory central to diasporic writing?
5. How does globalization influence literature?
6. What themes dominate Indian diasporic writing?

Long Answer Questions

1. Discuss displacement and belonging in diasporic literature.
2. Analyse identity formation in Indian diasporic writing.
3. Examine cultural memory in diaspora narratives.
4. How does globalization reshape Indian literary consciousness?
5. Diasporic literature as a cultural bridge-discuss.
6. Evaluate transnational Indian English writing.

9

Contemporary Indian English Literature – New Voices, New Directions

9.1 Expansion of Themes and Genres

Contemporary Indian English literature moves beyond traditional themes to include urban life, technology, youth culture, caste dynamics, and political unrest. Writers experiment with genres such as graphic fiction, speculative narratives, and popular fiction. English adapts to reflect rapidly changing Indian society.

Contemporary Indian English literature reflects a decisive shift from the limited thematic concerns of earlier periods to a much wider and more complex engagement with modern Indian realities. While earlier Indian English writing often focused on rural life, colonial encounters, nationalism, and traditional social structures, present-day writers address the lived experiences of a rapidly transforming society. Urbanization, globalization, migration, and technological change have reshaped Indian life, and literature in English has evolved accordingly to capture these new realities with greater immediacy and diversity.

One major expansion is the representation of **urban life**. Contemporary writers explore metropolitan spaces marked by anonymity, aspiration, inequality, and cultural fragmentation. Cities are portrayed not merely as physical settings but as psychological landscapes where individuals negotiate ambition, alienation, and identity. Alongside this, **youth culture** has emerged as a prominent theme. Writers depict young Indians grappling with career pressures, relationships, consumer culture, and the influence of global media, presenting identity as fluid rather than fixed.

Another significant development is the direct engagement with **technology and digital culture**. Mobile phones, social media, surveillance, and virtual relationships appear as integral elements of modern narratives. These themes highlight how technology reshapes communication, intimacy, and power structures, often blurring the boundary between private and public life. Literature thus becomes a space to critically examine both the possibilities and anxieties of digital modernity.

Contemporary Indian English literature also confronts **caste dynamics, political unrest, and social injustice** with greater urgency and openness. Writers address marginalized voices, question entrenched hierarchies, and explore the intersections of caste, class, gender, and power. This thematic expansion reflects a growing ethical responsibility within literature to engage with social realities rather than merely aesthetic concerns.

Aspect	Traditional Focus (Earlier Indian English Writing)	Expanded Focus in Contemporary Indian English Literature
Social Setting	Rural life, village communities, colonial society	Urban spaces, metropolitan life, migration, globalized cities
Core Themes	Nationalism, tradition, family values, cultural identity	Youth culture, technology, caste dynamics, political unrest
Representation of Society	Generalized social concerns, symbolic portrayal	Lived realities, marginalized voices, intersection of caste, class, and gender
Role of Technology	Largely absent or peripheral	Central to narratives: social media, digital life, virtual identities
Treatment of Identity	Stable and tradition-bound identity	Fluid, evolving identity shaped by globalization and mobility
Genres Used	Novel, short story, lyric poetry	Graphic fiction, speculative fiction, crime fiction, popular literature
Narrative Style	Linear storytelling, realist approach	Experimental forms, hybrid genres, non-linear narratives
Purpose of Literature	Cultural representation and moral reflection	Social critique, experimentation, and engagement with contemporary change

In terms of form, there is notable experimentation with **genres**. Alongside the novel and short story, writers now embrace graphic fiction, speculative and dystopian narratives, crime fiction, fantasy, and popular literature. These genres allow authors to reach wider audiences and to explore complex issues through innovative narrative strategies. Speculative fiction, for instance, enables indirect critique of present conditions by imagining alternative futures or exaggerated realities.

Overall, the expansion of themes and genres demonstrates how English has adapted as a flexible and expressive medium for Indian writers. Rather than being a borrowed language, English is reshaped to reflect contemporary Indian consciousness, making modern Indian English literature dynamic, inclusive, and deeply responsive to social change.

9.2 Regional Voices in a Global Language

Modern writers increasingly bring regional experiences into English writing. Dialects, cultural practices, and local histories enrich narratives without translation loss. This trend challenges the idea that English writing is detached from grassroots reality.

Contemporary Indian English literature increasingly serves as a platform for expressing **regional experiences and local realities** , challenging the earlier perception that English writing in India is elite, urban, or disconnected from grassroots life. Modern writers consciously root their narratives in specific regions, communities, and cultural contexts, demonstrating that English can effectively convey the diversity of Indian life without diluting its authenticity.

One important feature of this trend is the **integration of regional dialects, speech patterns, and idioms** into English prose. Writers often retain native words, phrases, and cultural references, allowing the rhythm and flavour of local languages to shape the English narrative. Instead of translating everything into standardized English, authors trust readers to engage with unfamiliar terms through context. This approach preserves cultural nuance and avoids the loss of meaning that often occurs through direct translation.

Regional customs, rituals, food habits, landscapes, and social structures also play a central role in shaping these narratives. Whether depicting coastal communities, hill towns, desert regions, or small villages, writers use detailed local settings to ground their stories in lived experience. These regional elements do not function as mere background details; they actively influence characters' identities, conflicts, and worldviews.

Another significant aspect is the focus on local histories and marginalized communities. Writers bring attention to voices historically excluded from mainstream narratives-such as lower-caste groups, tribal populations, and economically disadvantaged regions. By telling their stories in English, authors ensure that regional struggles and histories reach both national and global audiences, expanding the scope and responsibility of Indian English literature.

This literary practice directly challenges the assumption that English is detached from Indian grassroots reality . Instead, English emerges as a flexible, adaptive medium capable of carrying regional authenticity. It becomes a bridge rather than a barrier-connecting local experiences with global readerships while retaining cultural specificity.

9.3 Digital Age and Literary Expression

The digital era has transformed literary production and readership. Blogs, online magazines, and social media platforms enable emerging voices to publish in English without traditional gatekeeping. This democratization expands representation and redefines authorship.

The digital age has significantly reshaped both the creation and circulation of Indian English literature, marking a shift from traditional, institution-driven publishing to more open and participatory modes of literary expression. Earlier, literary recognition largely depended on established publishers, academic circles, and print journals, which often limited access for writers outside elite or urban backgrounds. Digital platforms have disrupted this structure by offering alternative spaces where writers can share their work directly with readers.

Blogs, online magazines, e-journals, and social media platforms now function as important literary spaces. These platforms allow emerging writers to publish poetry, short fiction, essays, and experimental forms in English without the need for formal approval from publishers or editors. As a result, English writing in India has become more inclusive, reflecting a wider range of social, regional, and cultural experiences.

The digital medium has also **redefined authorship and literary identity** . Writers are no longer dependent solely on printed books to establish credibility. Online visibility, reader engagement, and community recognition contribute to a writer's literary presence. Readers, in turn, actively respond through comments, shares, and discussions, creating an interactive relationship between author and audience. This interaction influences themes, styles, and even language use, making literature more dynamic and responsive to contemporary realities.

Another key impact of the digital age is the **expansion of representation** . Voices from non-elite, regional, and marginalized backgrounds gain visibility through online platforms, challenging long-standing hierarchies in Indian English literature. Personal narratives, social critiques, and experimental forms flourish in these spaces, reflecting lived experiences often overlooked in mainstream publishing.

9.4 English as an Indian Language of the Future

Contemporary literature confirms that English is no longer an external or elite language in India. It has become an Indian language shaped by local realities and aspirations. The future of Indian English literature lies in its diversity, adaptability, and ability to reflect evolving consciousness.

Contemporary Indian English literature clearly demonstrates that English in India is no longer a foreign, imposed, or exclusively elite language. Over decades of sustained literary use, English has been absorbed into the Indian linguistic environment and reshaped by indigenous thought patterns, social realities, and cultural experiences. Rather than standing apart from Indian life, English now functions as a language through which Indian aspirations, conflicts, and identities are authentically expressed.

Modern writers use English with an unmistakably Indian sensibility. Vocabulary, sentence rhythm, imagery, and narrative logic often reflect local languages and cultural frameworks. Indian social relationships, belief systems, humour, emotional expression, and moral dilemmas flow naturally into English prose and poetry. This adaptation shows that English has undergone a process of localization, evolving into a medium that carries Indian meanings rather than merely Western linguistic norms.

The growing accessibility of education, digital media, and global communication has further strengthened English as a shared language across regions, classes, and communities. Writers from diverse backgrounds-urban and rural, privileged and marginalized-use English to narrate their lived experiences. As a result, Indian English literature today is marked by **plurality rather than uniformity** . There is no single "Indian English voice," but many voices shaped by region, caste, gender, generation, and social context.

Looking ahead, the future of Indian English literature lies in its **diversity and adaptability**. As Indian society continues to change due to technological growth, social movements, environmental challenges, and shifting cultural values, English remains flexible enough to respond to these transformations. It allows writers to engage simultaneously with local realities and global audiences, making Indian experiences visible on an international stage without losing cultural depth.

In this sense, English has become an Indian language of the future-not because it replaces regional languages, but because it coexists with them as a complementary medium. Indian English literature will continue to thrive as long as it reflects evolving consciousness, embraces multiple identities, and remains rooted in the lived realities of Indian society.

9.5 Plural Voices and the Expanding Horizons of Indian English Literature

The future of Indian English literature lies in its increasing plurality of voices and perspectives. As English continues to evolve as an Indian language, it is no longer confined to urban, metropolitan, or elite narratives.

Writers from diverse regions, socio-economic backgrounds, genders, and professions are adopting English to articulate experiences that were earlier marginalized or unheard. This expansion reflects a shift from a narrow literary tradition to a broad, inclusive cultural space where multiple Indias coexist and converse.

Indian English literature is now shaped by regional realities and hybrid identities. Authors draw from local histories, folk traditions, oral narratives, and contemporary social challenges, blending them seamlessly into English expression. The language adapts to convey rural life, small-town aspirations, diasporic tensions, technological change, and grassroots movements. This adaptability ensures that English does not erase cultural specificity but becomes a medium through which local identities gain wider visibility.

Table 9.5: Emerging Dimensions of Indian English Literature

Dimension	Earlier Phase	Contemporary/Future Phase	Literary Impact
Authorial Voices	Limited, elite, urban	Diverse, regional, inclusive	Broader representation of Indian society
Cultural Sources	Colonial and Western influence	Local traditions, hybrid identities	Stronger cultural rootedness
Dominant Themes	Identity, nationalism, postcolonialism	Technology, environment, social justice	Expanded thematic relevance
Language Style	Formal, standardized English	Hybrid, localized English	Greater authenticity and accessibility
Publishing Access	Traditional, limited outlets	Digital and global platforms	Increased experimentation and reach

Another defining feature of this expanding horizon is thematic diversification. Contemporary and future Indian English writing increasingly engages with issues such as climate change, digital citizenship, mental health, gender fluidity, migration, and social justice. These themes reflect a changing national consciousness and position Indian English literature as a responsive and forward-looking body of work. English, in this context, serves as a flexible tool capable of addressing both deeply rooted social concerns and emerging global realities.

Importantly, the democratization of publishing platforms—through digital media, self-publishing, and global readerships—has further strengthened English as an Indian language of the future. Writers are no longer dependent solely on traditional gatekeepers. This openness allows experimentation in form, genre, and style, reinforcing the idea that Indian English literature is not static but continuously evolving alongside society.

Overall, English in India's literary future is not defined by uniformity but by diversity. Its strength lies in its capacity to hold contradictions, multiple voices, and layered identities. As Indian English literature moves forward, it will continue to function as a dynamic space where local realities meet global conversations, ensuring its relevance, vitality, and cultural authenticity.

Multiple Choice Questions (MCQs)

1. Contemporary Indian English literature differs from earlier phases mainly because it

A. Rejects Indian themes entirely

B. Focuses only on rural life

C. Expands themes to include modern social realities

D. Avoids experimentation in form

Answer: C

2. Which of the following themes is most commonly associated with contemporary Indian English literature?

A. Mythological retellings only

B. Courtly romance

C. Urban life and youth culture

D. Purely colonial experiences

Answer: C

3. The inclusion of caste dynamics and political unrest in modern writing reflects

A. Decline of literary quality

B. Writers' engagement with social realities

C. Influence of Western literature only

D. Rejection of Indian culture

Answer: B

4. The use of regional dialects and local expressions in English writing mainly aims to

A. Make texts difficult to understand

B. Eliminate regional languages

C. Preserve cultural authenticity

D. Standardize Indian English

Answer: C

5. How has the digital age influenced Indian English literature?

A. By reducing readership

B. By restricting publication to print media

C. By democratizing literary expression

D. By discouraging young writers

Answer: C

Short Answer Questions

1. What new themes appear in contemporary Indian English literature?
2. How has digital media changed literary expression?
3. Why are regional voices significant today?
4. What new genres are emerging?
5. How is English perceived in modern India?
6. What characterizes contemporary Indian writers?

Long Answer Questions

1. Discuss the changing themes of contemporary Indian English literature.
2. Analyse the impact of technology on literary production.
3. Examine the rise of regional narratives in English.
4. How has English become an Indian language of the future?
5. Evaluate contemporary literature as a mirror of modern India.
6. Discuss future directions of Indian English literature.

References

Chapter 1: English and the Indian Mind – A Historical Encounter

1. Macaulay, T. B. (1835). *Minute on Indian Education*. Government of India Archives.
2. Viswanathan, G. (1989). *Masks of Conquest: Literary Study and British Rule in India*. Oxford University Press.
3. Said, E. W. (1993). *Culture and Imperialism*. Vintage Books.

Chapter 2: Language, Identity, and Cultural Negotiation

1. Ashcroft, B., Griffiths, G., & Tiffin, H. (2002). *The Empire Writes Back: Theory and Practice in Post-Colonial Literatures*. Routledge.
2. Hall, S. (1996). *Cultural Identity and Diaspora*. In *Identity: Community, Culture, Difference*. Lawrence & Wishart.
3. Raja Rao. (1938). *Kanchipuram* (Author's Preface). Oxford University Press.

Chapter 3: Indian Sensibility in English Prose

1. Iyengar, K. R. S. (1985). *Indian Writing in English*. Sterling Publishers.
2. Mukherjee, M. (1971). *The Twice Born Fiction*. Heinemann.
3. Narasimhaiah, C. D. (1987). *The Swan and the Eagle*. Indian Institute of Advanced Study.

Chapter 4: Poetry in English and the Indian Inner World

1. King, B. (2001). *Modern Indian Poetry in English*. Oxford University Press.
2. Ramanujan, A. K. (1999). *The Collected Poems of A. K. Ramanujan*. Oxford University Press.
3. Mehrotra, A. K. (2003). *A History of Indian Literature in English*. Columbia University Press.

Chapter 5: Indian Drama in English – Stage as Social Conscience

1. Karnad, G. (2001). *Collected Plays*. Oxford University Press.
2. Dharwadker, A. (2005). *Theatres of Independence: Drama, Theory, and Urban Performance in India*. University of Iowa Press.
3. Naik, M. K., & Narayan, S. (2009). *Indian English Drama*. Prestige Books.

Chapter 6: Postcolonial Rewriting and Resistance

1. Fanon, F. (1963). *The Wretched of the Earth*. Grove Press.
2. Spivak, G. C. (1988). "Can the Subaltern Speak?" *Marxism and the Interpretation of Culture*. University of Illinois Press.
3. Bhabha, H. K. (1994). *The Location of Culture*. Routledge.

Chapter 7: Feminist Voices and Gendered Consciousness

1. Showalter, E. (1977). *A Literature of Their Own*. Princeton University Press.
2. Desai, A. (1980). *Clear Light of Day*. Vintage International.
3. Roy, A. (1997). *The God of Small Things*. IndiaInk.

Chapter 8: Diaspora, Globalization, and Transnational Indian English

1. Rushdie, S. (1991). *Imaginary Homelands*. Granta Books.
2. Lahiri, J. (2003). *The Namesake*. Houghton Mifflin.
3. Brah, A. (1996). *Cartographies of Diaspora*. Routledge.

Chapter 9: Contemporary Indian English Literature – New Voices, New Directions

1. Nayar, P. K. (2015). *Contemporary Indian Literature in English*. Pearson.
2. Ghosh, A. (2004). *The Shadow Lines*. Penguin India.
3. Mehrotra, A. K. (Ed.). (2012). *A Concise History of Indian Literature in English*. Permanent Black.

APPENDIX

1. Glossary of Key Terms

Colonial Discourse

The body of texts, ideas, and representations produced during colonial rule that shaped perceptions of colonized societies and justified imperial dominance.

Cultural Hybridity

The blending of indigenous cultural elements with foreign influences, resulting in new and complex forms of identity and expression.

Diaspora Literature

Literary works produced by writers living outside their ancestral homeland, often focusing on migration, displacement, memory, and identity.

Feminist Literary Criticism

An approach to literature that examines representations of women, gender relations, and power structures, emphasizing women's voices and experiences.

Indianization of English

The process by which English is adapted to reflect Indian thought patterns, idioms, cultural references, and social realities.

Postcolonial Literature

Literature produced in formerly colonized societies that critiques colonial power structures and reclaims cultural identity.

Subaltern

Groups or individuals marginalized within social, political, or cultural hierarchies whose voices are often excluded from dominant narratives.

Transnational Identity

An identity shaped by connections across national boundaries, often seen in diasporic and globalized literary contexts.

2. Data Sources and Datasets

Although literary studies rely primarily on textual analysis rather than numerical datasets, the following **authoritative sources** support research and academic inquiry:

- **University Libraries and Digital Archives** – British Library, National Library of India
- **Academic Databases** – JSTOR, Project MUSE, Google Scholar
- **Literary Anthologies** – Sahitya Akademi publications, Oxford and Penguin Indian English literature series
- **Government and Institutional Reports** – Educational records on colonial education and language policy
- **Author Archives and Interviews** – Published interviews, speeches, and essays by Indian English writers

These sources provide **primary texts, historical context, and critical commentary** essential for literary analysis.

3. Tools and Frameworks

Postcolonial Theory

Used to analyse power relations, resistance, hybridity, and identity formation in Indian English literature.

Feminist Theory

Applied to examine gendered narratives, representation of women, and patriarchal structures in texts.

Cultural Studies Approach

Focuses on literature as a reflection of social, political, and cultural processes rather than isolated artistic expression.

Comparative Literary Analysis

Compares Indian English texts with British, regional Indian, or global literature to highlight distinctive consciousness.

Narrative and Discourse Analysis

Examines storytelling techniques, voice, language use, and ideological positioning within texts.

4. References for Further Reading

i. Mehrotra, A. K. *A History of Indian Literature in English*. Columbia University Press.

ii. Naik, M. K. *A History of Indian English Literature*. Sahitya Akademi.

iii. Nayar, P. K. *Postcolonial Literature: An Introduction*. Pearson.

iv. Ashcroft, B., Griffiths, G., & Tiffin, H. *The Empire Writes Back*. Routledge.

v. Tharu, S., & Lalita, K. *Women Writing in India*. Oxford University Press.

vi. King, B. *Modern Indian Poetry in English*. Oxford University Press.

These texts deepen understanding of **language, identity, resistance, gender, and globalization** in Indian English literature.

5. Future Directions in Indian English Literary Studies

Future research may focus on emerging voices from marginalized regions and communities, expanding the scope of Indian English literature beyond elite narratives. Digital literature, social media storytelling, and multilingual experimentation will reshape literary expression. Interdisciplinary approaches combining literature with sociology, media studies, and digital humanities will offer new insights. The growing acceptance of English as an Indian language suggests a future where literature reflects plural identities, social justice concerns, and evolving global realities without cultural erasure.

6. Summary of Key Points

- English in India has evolved from a colonial language into a medium of cultural self-expression.
- Indian English literature reflects identity negotiation, resistance, and hybridity.

ABOUT THE AUTHOR

Dr. Jyoti Devi is a dedicated English educator and researcher with a strong academic foundation and a sustained commitment to language teaching and literary studies. She holds a PhD in English from Himalayan Garhwal University, where her research focused on critical and pedagogical dimensions of English literature and language education. She completed her Master of Arts in English from Indira Gandhi National Open University (IGNOU) in 2015, securing Grade A, and earned her Bachelor's degree in History from Periyar University in 2010, reflecting her interdisciplinary academic background. With a passion for teaching, Dr. Jyoti Devi has been actively engaged in fostering critical thinking, communication skills, and literary appreciation among students. Her academic interests include English literature, language pedagogy, and interdisciplinary humanities research. She is proficient in Hindi and English, enabling her to connect effectively with diverse learners. Dr. Jyoti Devi continues to contribute to academia through teaching, research, and scholarly engagement, with a focus on nurturing linguistic competence and intellectual curiosity.

10. E-LIBRAIRIE – France (French online bookstore)
11. Everand – India (Everand Book Distributor is based in India)
12. EXLIBRIS – Switzerland
13. Fable – United Kingdom (UK/Europe digital subscription book service)
14. Flipkart – India
15. GANDHI.com – Mexico (Librerías Gandhi)
16. Google Book – United States (Google LLC)
17. Google Audio Book – United States (Google LLC)
18. IBS.IT – Italy Wikipedia
19. Indigo – Canada
20. Kobo – Canada Wikipedia
21. Kindle – United States (Amazon product)
22. LAFELTRINELLI – Italy Wikipedia
23. Lehmanns – Germany
24. Lulu – United States
25. MORAWA – Austria
26. Rakuten Japan – Japan (Rakuten)
27. Smashwords – United States
28. Tolino / Thalia – Germany (Tolino is a German-language eBook ecosystem, Thalia DE)

29. Vivlio – France

30. Saxo – Denmark (Saxo.com)

31. YES24 – South Korea

and others.

🎁 You will receive 20 physical author copies FREE to your Indian address.

⭐ You can also receive 5 book reviews:

* 3 reviews by eminent university professors

* 2 reviews from your own group/colleagues/seniors/teachers

www.books.wissira.us

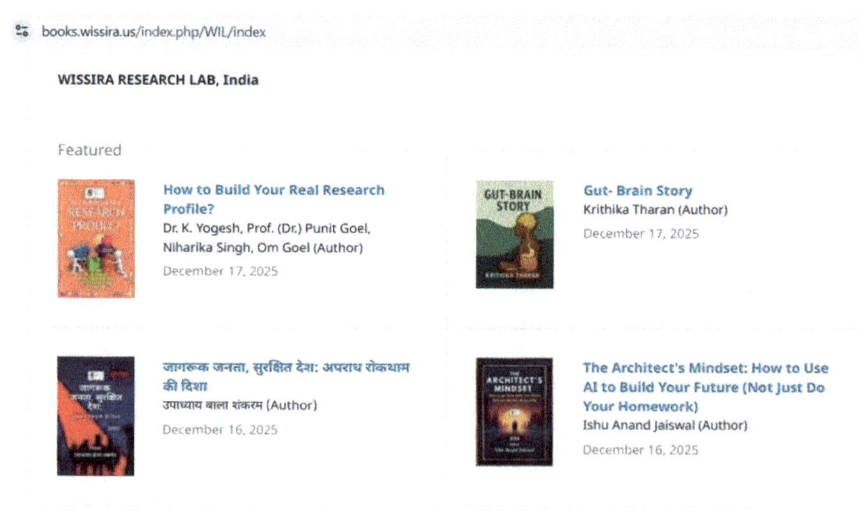

www.books.wissira.us

DOI: https://doi.org/10.63345/book.wrl.2512000324

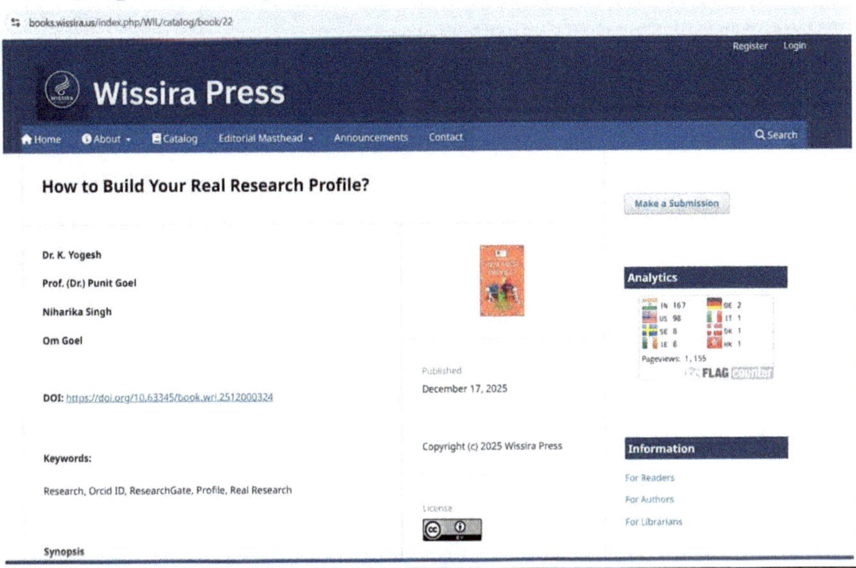

https://books.wissira.us/index.php/WIL/login

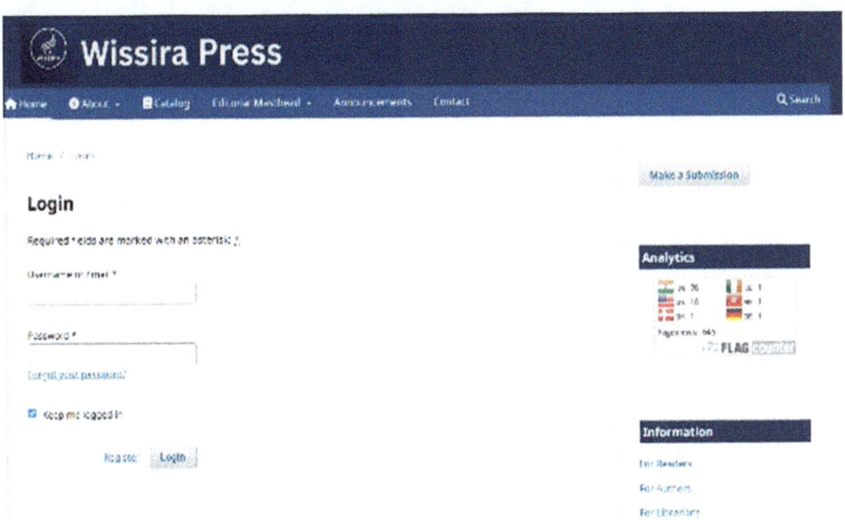

https://books.wissira.us/index.php/WIL/catalog

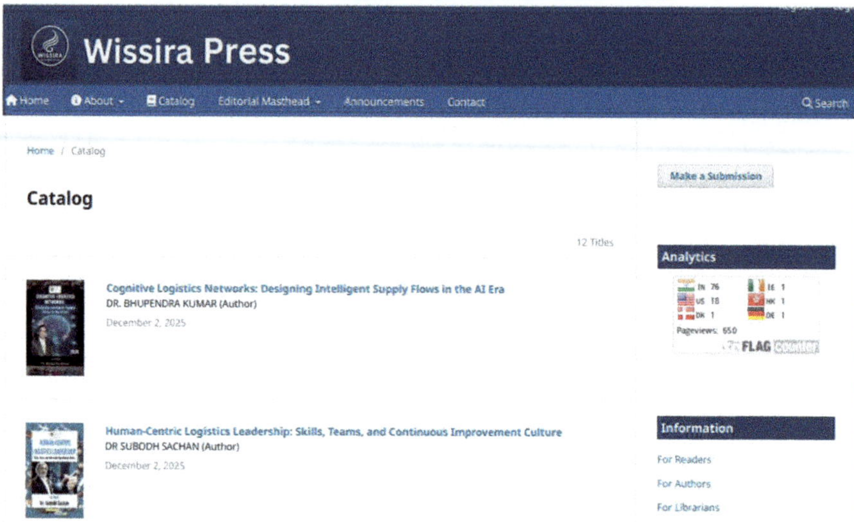

https://books.wissira.us/index.php/WIL/about/contact

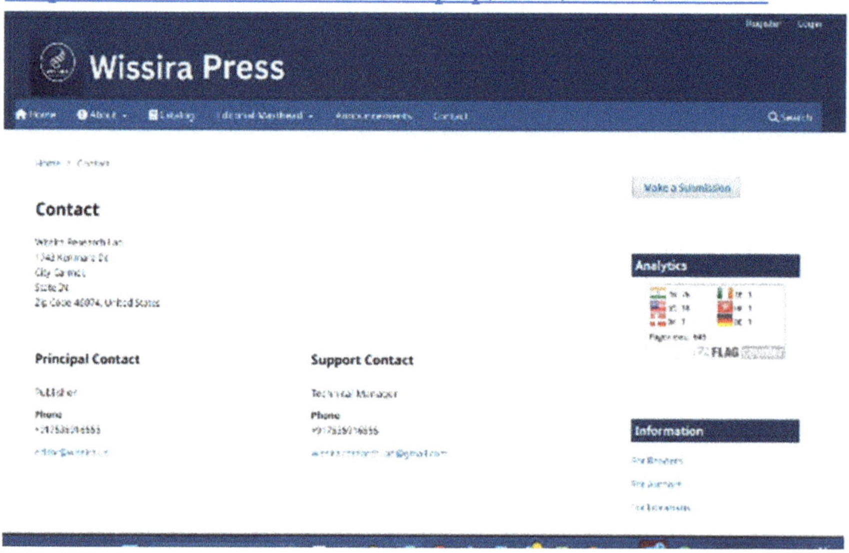

https://www.amazon.in/dp/B0G7MQFD2L

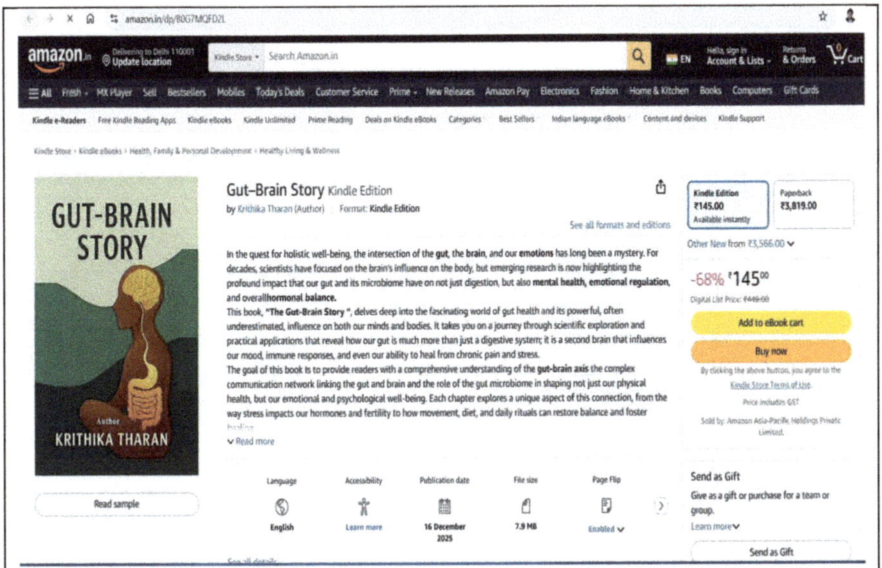

https://books.apple.com/us/book/the-architects-mindset-how-to-use-ai-to-build-your/id6756545876

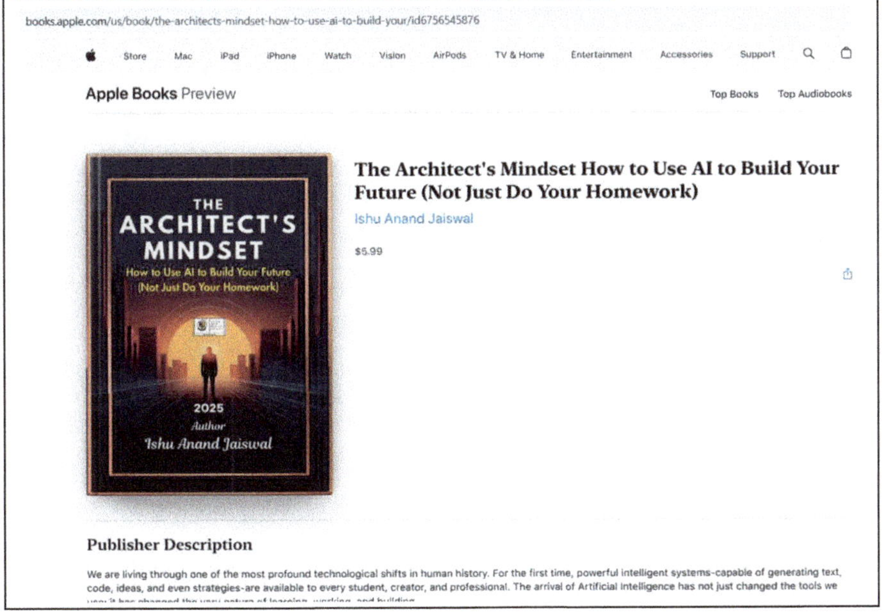

Flipkart:
https://tinyurl.com/WissieaPressBook250306Human

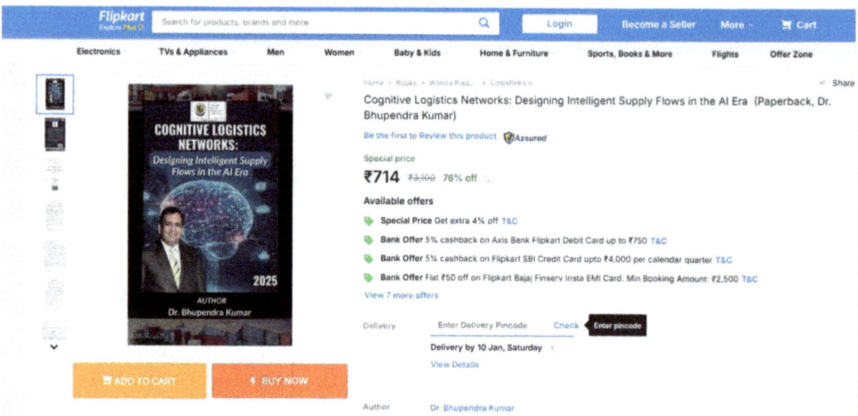

https://play.google.com/store/audiobooks/details?id=AQAAAEAa9DeoPM

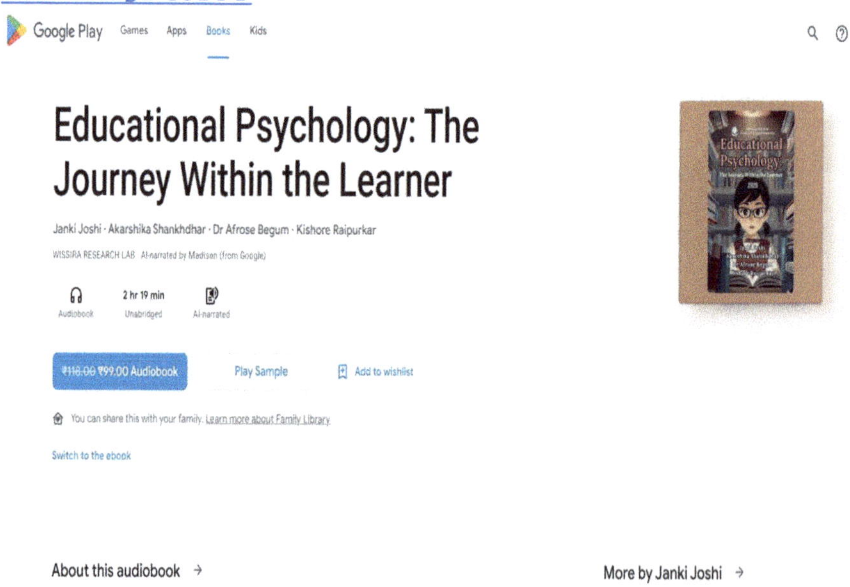

https://shop.vivlio.com/product/9798232547615_9798232547615_10020/human-centric-logistics-leadership-skills-teams-and-continuous-improvement-culture

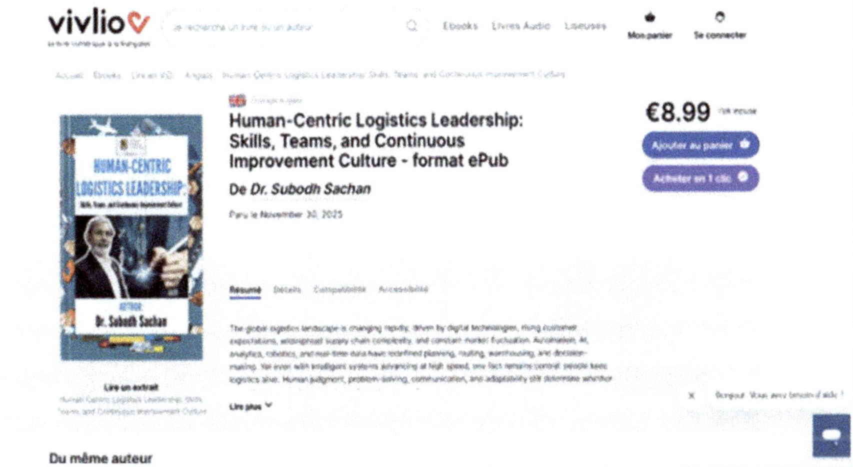

https://www.kobo.com/in/en/ebook/from-shakespeare-to-tagore-reinterpreting-english-literature-through-indian-sensibility?sId=070486d4-8aef-4220-a1d2-26bb2ba8ecb6&ssId=3FJLsnB4eTMdnS31kaTcM

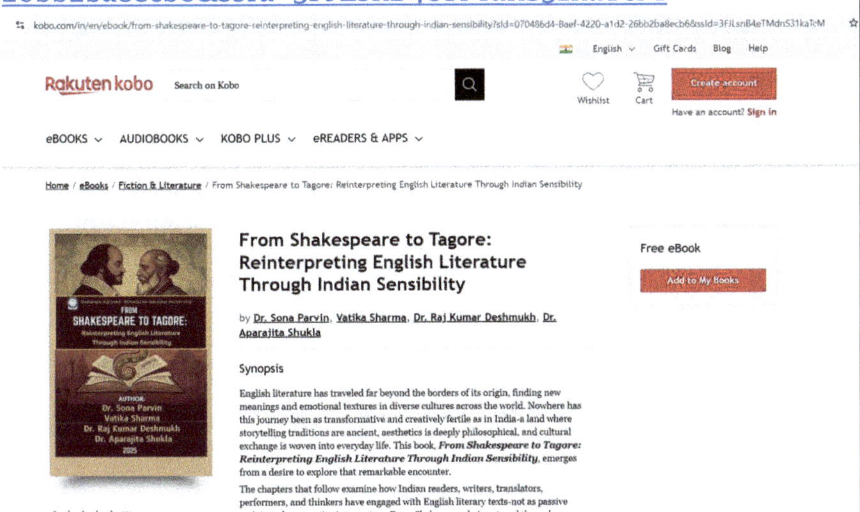

https://fable.co/book/x-9798230804772

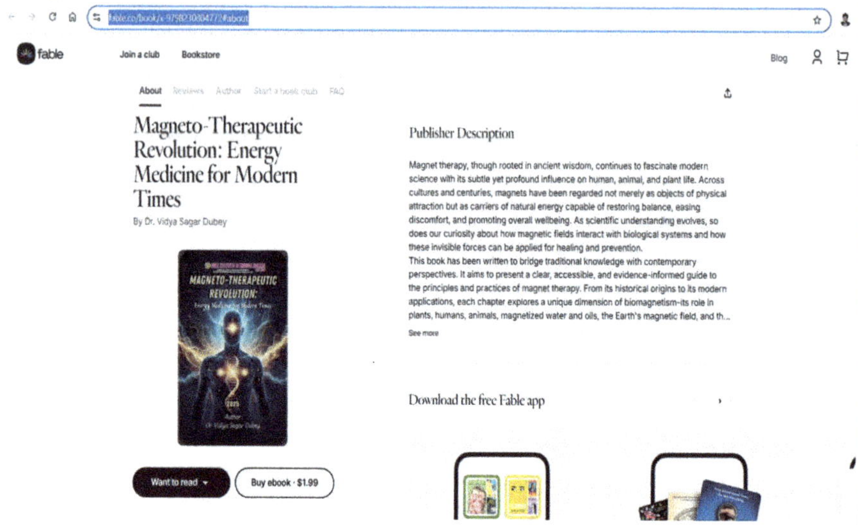

https://www.lulu.com/shop/dr-subodh-sachan/human-centric-logistics-leadership/ebook/product-rmj4erq.html?q=Human-Centric+Logistics+Leadership%3A+Skills%2C+Teams%2C+and+Continuous+Improvement+Culture&page=1&pageSize=

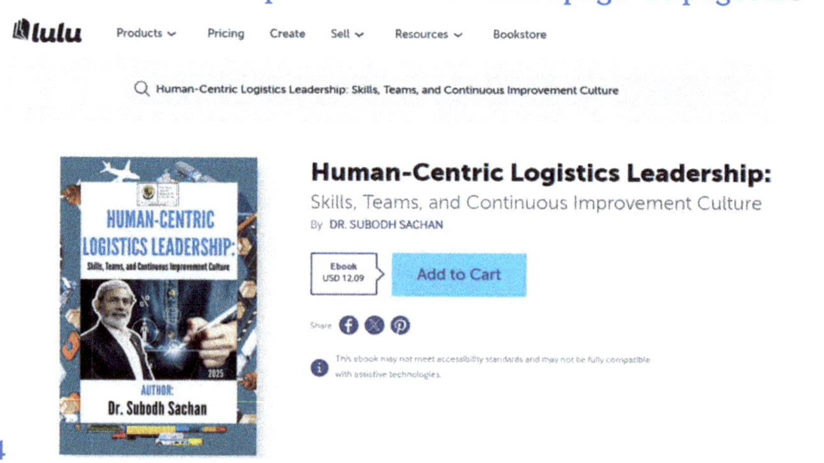

4

https://play.google.com/store/audiobooks/details?id=AQAAAEDqoRHh6M

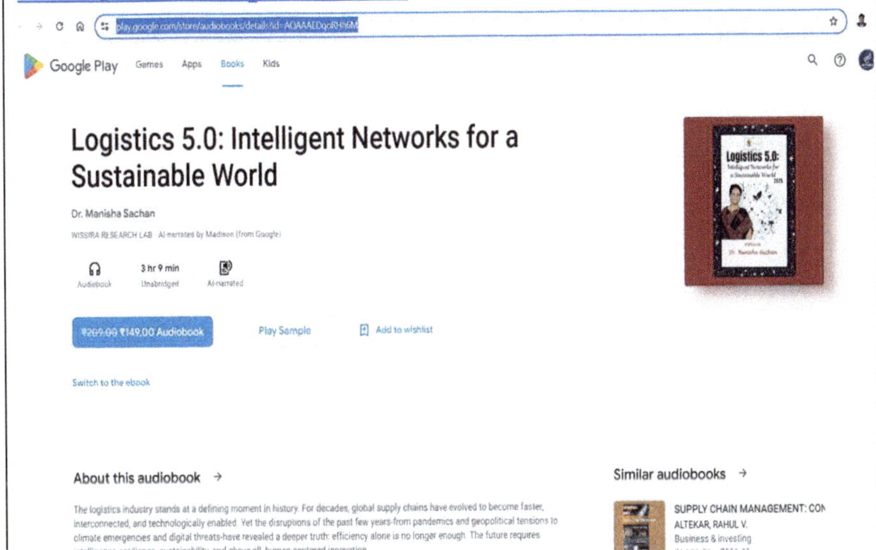

https://play.google.com/store/books/details?id=TbmfEQAAQBAJ

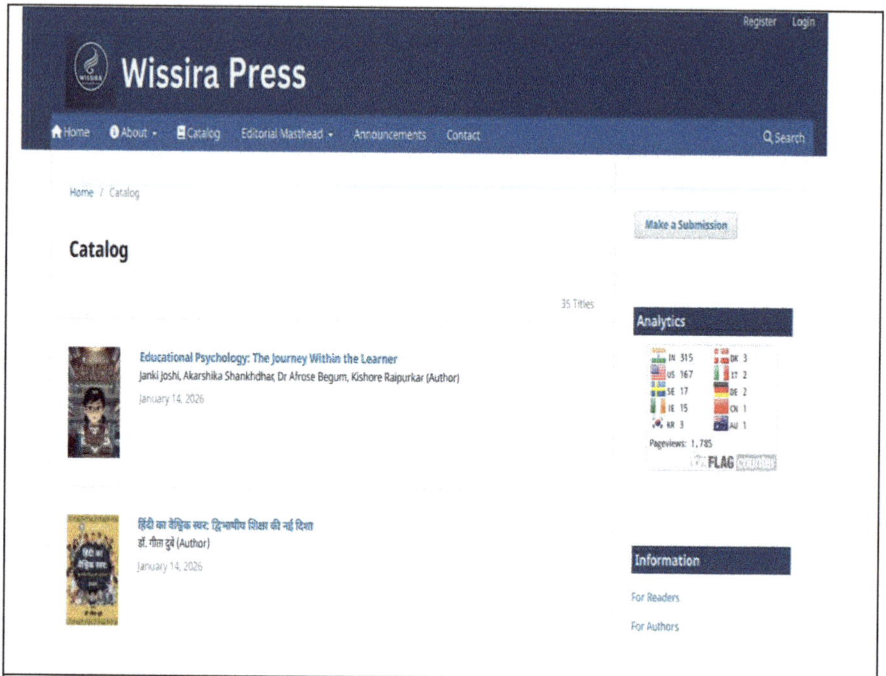

https://www.smashwords.com/books/view/1943936

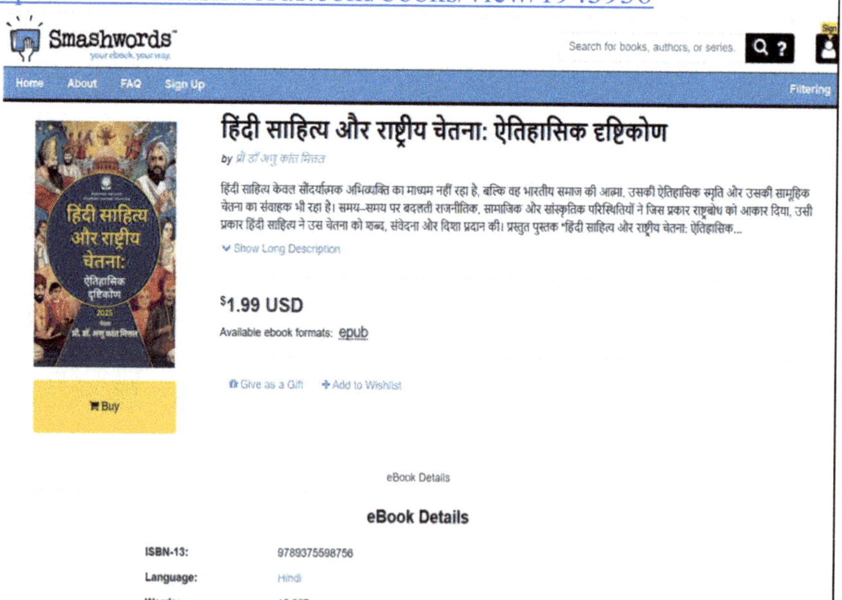

Amazon Kindle

Amazon

Flipkart

LULU

Apple Books

Barnes & Nobles

Everand

Fable

Kobo

Analytics

IN	135	IT	1
US	84	DK	1
SE	8	HK	1
IE	8	DE	1

Pageviews: 1,012

FLAG counter

Information

For Readers

For Authors

For Librarians

Keywords

sustain long-term operational excellence.

Across the nine chapters of this work, readers will find a structured and practical approach to understanding how leadership influences logistics outcomes. Beginning with the foundations of human-centric leadership, the book explores essential competencies such as communication, empathy, decision-making, and ethical responsibility-skills that enable leaders to build credibility and trust in high-pressure environments. It then moves deeper into the dynamics of teamwork, motivation, and empowerment, highlighting how resilient and collaborative teams become the backbone of

Smashwords

Tolino

Vivlio

Google Books

---

www.ingramcontent.com/pod-product-compliance
Ingram Content Group UK Ltd.
Pitfield, Milton Keynes, MK11 3LW, UK
UKHW021411190726
13845UKWH00028B/1018

9 789375 590903